D1329998

INTELLIGENT CHARISMATIC ®

Changing the way you think about your faith.

For more resources, please visit
intelligentcharismatic.com.

INTELLIGENT CHARISMATIC:
The Believer's Guide to a Spirit-Filled Life

MICHAEL D. WHITE

INTELLIGENT CHARISMATIC
New York

For information about special discounts for bulk purchases, please visit intelligentcharismatic.com.

For information about inviting Michael D. White to speak at a special event, please complete our booking form at intelligentcharismatic.com.

Cover design by Chris Rosenberry @ Fifth Story Interactive

ISBN 978-0-6929-0672-9

This book is dedicated to my wife. Rachael, you are the most beautiful, intelligent, and selflessly compassionate woman in the world. You have loved me through my best and worst moments, and supported me every step of the way. You encouraged me to finish this book when I didn't feel inspired, and helped me to wait in faith as God worked behind the scenes to publish it. This is not my work; it is ours. I love you with all my heart.

Thank you to Pastor Bojan Jancic for taking a long shot on a finance guy. You have trusted and supported me from day one, and it is an honor to serve you as we serve Jesus.

Thank you to Allison Armerding for giving new life to my ideas, and expressing my thoughts better than I can express myself.

Finally, thank you to the members of CityLight Church. This book is the result of all the conversations we have had together. Your questions and comments inspire me to seek God for wisdom, and yearn to know Him more. I truly love and cherish our church family.

PRAISE FOR INTELLIGENT CHARISMATIC

Whether you are a new believer or you have been serving the Lord for a long time, this book will cause the joy of salvation and power of the Holy Spirit to become fresh and new all over again. In my opinion, The Believer's Guide to a Spirit-Filled Life should be a part of every local church's curriculum and every Spirit-filled believer's library.

David Wagner
Founder, Father's Heart Ministries
Pensacola, FL

The Sadducees didn't believe in the resurrection of the dead, angels or miracles. In Matthew 22 they ask Jesus a question regarding marriage at the resurrection, and Jesus' response was both profound and timeless: "Jesus replied, 'You are in error because you do not know the Scriptures or the power of God'" (Matt 22:29). The Sadducees weren't asking a question about the power of God; they were asking about Scripture. But I love how Jesus doesn't separate the two, and neither should we.

In the North American church we have been guilty of either being a "word" church or a "Spirit" church. Those from the "word" camp usually have a greater understanding of the context of scriptures, emphasizing the importance of having a solid biblical understanding and come from a more academic perspective. The "Spirit" churches are known for long worship services, moving in the gifts of the Spirit but often emphasize "feeling" more than understanding.

Pastor Michael White has brilliantly bridged a gap, and created a middle ground that will combine what he has coined, "Intelligent Charismatic." As Spirit-filled believers we don't have to be so open minded that our brains fall out. I believe in the pages of this book lies the blueprint for the reformation of the church that walks in the word and the Spirit.

Ivan Roman
Senior Leader, Empowered Life Church
Medford, OR

Jesus commands us to worship Him in "spirit and in truth" because He is Spirit (John 4:24). Our Christian walk is not a question of either/or but rather both/and more -- spirit and truth. Could Christians be naturally supernatural, yet also intelligent and intentional about their faith? How do we love God with all our heart, all our soul, all our mind and all our strength?

Pastor Michael White skillfully makes a well thought out and intentional case for why believers should live in the fullness of the Spirit. Jeremiah prophesies about God raising up "shepherds after His own heart" (Jer 3:15). Pastor Michael White is undoubtedly one of these shepherds who pursues both God's heart and people's hearts so well.

The following pages are the fruit of the way he loves people so intentionally. I have watched first-hand as Pastor Mike pastors New York City, loves his city well, and bridges both the secular and sacred worlds. I believe in him and believe that this book will take you on an encounter and an invitation into the "more" that Jesus died for.

Shara Pradhan
Producer, Writer & Director of *Compelled by Love*
Casting Director, iBethel TV
Redding, CA

These postmodern times demand prayerful and critical methodical thinking paradigms in order to reach populations of Christians who may be unaware of Christ in His totality. Pastor Michael White, as an intellectual charismatic integrationist, presents a powerful model to bridge the gap between charismatic and nominal Christians. Readers will become more spiritually encouraged, Biblically knowledgeable, and socially relevant – without being doctrinally dogmatic – as a result of this book. The Intelligent Charismatic will teach you to be unapologetically Christian yet culturally-engaging by speaking truth through intellect for power in Christ.

Dr. Marcia Lucas
Program Director, Manhattan Campus
Alliance Graduate School of Counseling
New York, NY

We've known Michael White and his wife, Rachael, for several years in our role as Northeast Regional Directors for the International Association of Healing Rooms. Michael and Rachael have been Directors of the CityLight Healing Rooms for years. Michael has a passion for the things of God, so much so that he left a lucrative career in investment banking to pursue a new career in the Kingdom of God. He is currently serving as Pastor, Healing Room Director and father. Michael never does things halfway; his passion for God and his pursuit of excellence will be evident throughout his book. In Intelligent Charismatic: The Believer's Guide to a Spirit-Filled Life, you will be challenged to examine your beliefs about healing, the supernatural, and all things God. We highly endorse Michael and his book. Enjoy it, and allow it to challenge you to grow in the grace and knowledge of the Lord Jesus Christ.

Vincent & Deborah Aquilino
New York State & Northwest Region Directors
International Association of Healing Rooms

TABLE OF CONTENTS

INTELLIGENT CHARISMATIC

FOREWORD

By David Wagner

In May 2015, I had the honor of meeting Pastor Mike White while ministering at City Light Church in New York City, where he serves as the Executive Pastor. My heart immediately felt connected to him as we fellowshipped, ministered, and shared meals together. I learned that Mike is a pastor who loves Jesus, is passionate about the presence of God, and really loves people. He has an amazing gift to equip believers by helping them discover their destiny and step into their identity as sons and daughters of God.

Pastor Mike has written more than just a brilliant book; he has created a roadmap that will help new believers become mature, Spirit-filled Christians. *The Believer's Guide to a Spirit-Filled Life* is a phenomenal tool that is sure to help you develop a strong foundation for your faith. Through his transparency and personal testimony, Mike imparts valuable wisdom for how to live out the normal Christian life. There is no doubt in my mind that this book is a much-needed tool for the body of Christ today. It is filled with revelation and wisdom that will lead you to discover the gifts, grace, and divine destiny that God has placed inside you.

One of the things I loved most about *The Believer's Guide* is that it takes a holistic approach to New Testament living. It helps you discover the Father's love and heart, the full-grown Jesus Christ who lives inside you, and the power of the Holy

Spirit. This book also removes the fear of stepping into the unknowns of church and the Christian life, all while helping you realize that the Holy Spirit does not make you weird—He makes you wonderful. Pastor Mike does an amazing job of making biblical principles come alive with clear applications for real life.

The Believer's Guide isn't just for new believers! This book is full of answers to the key questions almost every Christ follower has asked at some point in their journey of faith. As I read each chapter, I found myself thinking about how this guide would have helped me when I first came to faith. In fifteen years of global itinerant ministry, I have also frequently noticed a need throughout the body of Christ for the kind of practical and relevant teaching in this amazing book. The insights Pastor Mike brings out in each chapter and section will deepen your understanding of the gospel and the life into which it invites you—a life filled with the power of God and demonstrations of the Holy Spirit found in the New Testament Church.

Whether you are a new believer or you have been serving the Lord for a long time, this book will cause the joy of salvation and power of the Holy Spirit to become fresh and new all over again. In my opinion, *The Believer's Guide to a Spirit-Filled Life* should be a part of every local church's curriculum and every Spirit-filled believer's library.

David Wagner
Founder, Father's Heart Ministries
Pensacola, FL

MY TESTIMONY

The summer after I graduated from college, I moved to New York City to take a job as a trader at a major financial institution. I was twenty-two years old and had it all figured out...or so I thought.

Months after moving to the city, I felt lost and depressed. In a city of over *eight million people*, I felt alone. Growing up, I figured happiness was something that was guaranteed—that if I did everything I was "supposed to do" and followed all the rules, everything would just fall into place. My parents had made it look so easy!

I was wrong. I was making lots of money, but I was broke. I had a lot of friends, but I was alone. I was decent at meeting women (I am being generous here), but I couldn't keep a relationship.

One day, as my brother and I were talking on the phone, he let me have it. "You need to find a church you like and get involved," he said. "Stop fooling around, and stop wasting time."

That was exactly what I needed to hear. I Googled "New York City churches for young people," and found a church seven blocks from my apartment. The next Sunday, I was on my way.

Little did I know the church I had selected was a "Spirit-filled" church. I'll never forget the first time I walked in.

The people were young and friendly...almost *too* friendly. Yes, I was a first-time guest. No, I didn't want to give out my e-mail. I quietly found my seat and tried my best to avoid awkward conversation. I wasn't sure what to expect, and that made me nervous.

Worship started, and I was blown away. I actually liked the music! The band was well rehearsed, and I had even heard some of the songs before. But when I looked around, I began to feel uncomfortable. Things were starting to get *weird*.

Why are these people raising their hands? I thought. *This isn't one of "those churches," is it?*

Before I could finish my thought, somebody in front of me started shouting and jumping up and down.

Relax, I told myself. *You can leave after the next song if they don't settle down.*

After a few more verses and a chorus, the jumper was done. She sat down, exhausted and out of breath.

Thank God, I thought. *It's over.*

Then the tongues started. First, they were quiet. I attempted to ignore them and just listen to the music. Then they got louder. Before I knew it, some lady and her husband were *screaming in tongues* behind me.

"What is going *on*?" I muttered.

Never in my life had I experienced anything like what was happening in this church service. I had been raised in a Congregational church in New England. Our church was the big, white church with the big, white steeple, sitting in the center of the town square. I had visited a lot of other churches too. I thought I knew what Christianity was all about, and this was definitely not it. I had never even *heard* of tongues before, and I definitely hadn't spoken in them. I was raised to think that people raising their hands in worship meant one thing: this is a cult!

I left that church service early, shaken up and a little disturbed. By the time I got home to my apartment, I was feeling dazed and confused. The one thing I felt sure of was that I never wanted to go back to that church. They were getting it all wrong! That wasn't how people were supposed to worship. We were supposed to sit in the pew, close our eyes, and reflect *quietly*.

As the day progressed, however, I couldn't help trying to figure out what it was about that church service that made me so uncomfortable. Sometime that evening, it finally hit me. Part of me felt uncomfortable because, according to my upbringing, dancing, shouting, and praying in tongues were not valid expressions of Christian worship. But another part of me couldn't help wondering whether these people knew something I didn't. Could there be something in Christianity I hadn't experienced before—maybe even something Satan wanted to keep me *from*?

Eventually, I made a decision to push through my discomfort and come back to that church. I decided to give those "crazy Christians" the benefit of the doubt and find out for sure if there was more to Christianity that God wanted me to know about, even if it made me uncomfortable. I was determined to search the Scriptures to find out if these weird, foreign worship practices were valid or not. I was hungry enough for a deeper relationship with God to take the risk.

I soon discovered that everything I had experienced in that first church service was firmly based in Scripture. Even more importantly, I was introduced to Spirit-filled living—walking through life in genuine relationship with Jesus Christ, with God's Holy Spirit as my Guide. Eventually, I was baptized—first in water, and then in the Holy Spirit—and became a member. I never turned back. Years later, I am now a pastor at that same Spirit-filled church.

Searching for a Guide

If speaking in tongues makes you nervous, you are not alone. If the phrase "baptism in the Holy Spirit" makes you queasy, then I have been in your shoes. Let me state the obvious:

Charismatic Christianity can be a tough sell. "Spirit-filled" Christians can act pretty funny. What is more, we don't always do the best job of explaining *why* we speak in tongues, live prophetic lifestyles, and fall over when someone prays for us. If you come to a Spirit-filled church and you're unprepared, then it's likely that at best, you'll leave confused, and at worst, you'll leave convinced that you never want to come back. I know I was shaken by that first service—it was jarring, and I was alarmed.

I'm here to tell you to push through that initial discomfort. Keep searching the Scriptures, and keep asking questions. If you feel like your spiritual life has become dry and stale, *there is more*. There is a difference between knowing God exists, and knowing Him through His Son Jesus Christ. There is a difference between praying and wondering what God might say, and praying and hearing what God is saying through His Holy Spirit.

I'm also here to offer you something I didn't have when I began to explore Spirit-filled Christianity—a guide. Though I found a lot of good books for new believers, the subject matter was often the same: *Do better. Try harder. Read the Bible. Make good Christian friends.* None of them had what I was seeking. If I was going to speak in tongues, I wanted to know everything I could about the subject. If I was going to tithe, I wanted to know every verse in Scripture that talked about money. If I was going to raise my hands in worship and sing *loud* to God, I wanted to find my example in God's Word. I wrote this book to answer the most common questions I had about Spirit-filled Christianity as a new believer. My hope is that it will help you navigate the waters of embracing a life with God's Holy Spirit as your Guide.

CHAPTER 1

THE GOSPEL

For no other foundation can anyone lay
than that which is laid, which is Jesus Christ.

1 Corinthians 3:11

This book is built on the premise that the Christian life is the Spirit-*filled* life, the Spirit-*led* life, and the Spirit-*gifted* life. Life in the Spirit is not something added to the gospel; it is life ushered in by the gospel. As we embark on exploring this Spirit-filled Christian life together, then, the best place to begin is by taking a fresh look at the Gospel message.

In a world of sound bites, we commonly find the gospel message reduced to one-liners, slogans, or formulas:

"Jesus saves."

"Jesus took what you deserve so you could get what He deserves."

"Jesus paid the price for your sin."

"If you confess your sins and put your trust in Jesus, you'll be forgiven and go to heaven when you die."

While these are true, we cannot reduce the gospel to a formula. The gospel is a reality that is simple enough for a child to understand and receive, yet one that must be understood and experienced ever more deeply as you progress along your journey with Jesus. It is the foundation of faith, but it is a foundation that must grow as you grow. As Spirit-filled believers, we must continually return to this core reality that is to define everything about us.

What Is Our Problem?

The gospel means "good news." In fact, it's the *best* news. One of the signs you're actually "getting" what the gospel really means is that you start to think, *That's so good, it's hard to believe. It feels too good to be true.* If a good God came up with the gospel, then it shouldn't surprise us that it is better than anything we could have invented on our own!

However, plenty of people perceive the gospel to be irrelevant news at best, and bad news at worst, because of where the message starts. It starts by announcing that every human on the planet has a fatal problem that none of us can possibly fix. What is that problem? According to the gospel, the problem with the human race is not war, tyranny, injustice, racism, slavery, sex trafficking, or some other social evil. Those are all just the fruit of the same root, which is *sin*.

Sin means "to miss the mark."[1] The word implies there is a standard to be met, and that standard is the way in which God, our Creator, designed us to live. God's purpose in creating humanity was nothing less than inviting an entire race of beloved sons and daughters to freely share in the abundant life, joy, and love of God Himself. Thus, He created us "in His image"[2] to imitate and reflect His very nature and character. Instead of honoring God's design, however, we violated it. We refused to trust our Maker, refused to listen to His instructions for how to live, and refused to be who He created us to be.

So why is sin such a big deal? Because "the wages of sin is death" (Romans 6:23). We typically think of death as the moment our souls leave our bodies or we cease to exist, but Biblical truth goes deeper than that. Man, being made in the

---

[1] See Strong's H2398 "chata'", Strong's G266 "hamartia"

[2] Then God said, "Let Us make man in Our image, according to Our likeness; let them have dominion over the fish of the sea, over the birds of the air, and over the cattle, over all the earth and over every creeping thing that creeps on the earth." – Genesis 1:26

image of God, who is Spirit, is also spirit. In essence, each of us is a spirit who possesses a soul and lives in a body.[3] Before sin entered the world, humans (Adam and Eve) enjoyed direct Spirit-to-spirit connection with God and shared His life. Sin destroyed that connection, and this spiritual separation from God is what makes us "dead in our sins."[4] According to the Bible, our spiritual death is responsible not only for our physical death, but also for the "Pandora's box" of suffering we experience in this world—everything from painful childbirth to relational strife, sickness, disease, poverty, and oppression.

God could have swept sinful, spiritually dead humanity from the planet and started fresh, but He didn't. Instead, He initiated a cosmic rescue mission that would unfold throughout history and reveal His perfect love and perfect holiness in the most brilliant and stunning way.

The first stage of this mission was to call out an entire nation—the Jewish people—and establish them as His people by making a covenant with them. This covenant was an agreement in which God promised to bless and care for His people as long as they promised to honor His requirements—the Law—which included a moral code (the Ten Commandments) and guidelines for their cultural and religious life (everything from dietary restrictions to the celebration of annual fasts and feasts).

This covenant (we usually call it the Old Covenant) served several purposes. First, it revealed God's desire to have relationship with His people. Second, it revealed His perfect, holy standard for that relationship. And third, it ultimately revealed that human beings—even human beings with the best moral education—could not live up to God's standard. The Old

---

[3] Now may the God of peace Himself sanctify you completely; and may your whole spirit, soul, and body be preserved blameless at the coming of our Lord Jesus Christ. – 1 Thessalonians 5:23

[4] And you He made alive, who were dead in trespasses and sins… – Ephesians 2:1

Testament records how generation after generation of God's people tried and failed to keep His covenant.

If the story stopped here, we might think that God had either painted Himself into a corner or was playing some kind of cruel joke. Why would God pursue relationship with people who were incapable of honoring His standard? Why would He take such pains to teach them this standard if He knew they could never meet it?

Thankfully, the story did not end there. The Old Covenant, God revealed, was never meant to be the final solution to the problem of sin and death. It was only meant to diagnose the problem and offer a temporary solution that would point to the true, permanent solution: a New (and better!) Covenant.[5] The prophet Jeremiah foretold God's plan to establish this New Covenant with His people:

> *"Behold, the days are coming, says the LORD, when I will make a new covenant with the house of Israel and with the house of Judah...I will put My law in their minds, and write it on their hearts; and I will be their God, and they shall be My people. No more shall every man teach his neighbor, and every man his brother, saying, 'Know the LORD,' for they all shall know Me, from the least of them to the greatest of them, says the LORD. For I will forgive their iniquity, and their sin I will remember no more." —Jeremiah 31:31-34*

This New Covenant would succeed in doing three things the Old Covenant revealed were necessary, but could not accomplish:

1. God's standard (the Law) would no longer be external and unreachable for us, but integrated in

---

[5] But now He has obtained a more excellent ministry, inasmuch as He is also Mediator of a better covenant, which was established on better promises. – Hebrews 8:6

our thinking, emotions, and behavior ("written on our minds and hearts").

2. We would have direct, personal knowledge of God (even without priests and other mediators).

3. We would receive the full forgiveness and removal of our sin.

So how was God to accomplish these things? How was He to fully remove sin and its consequences—death—once and for all? How was He to restore our spiritual connection with Him and enable us to reflect His nature?

The only way God could make this New Covenant with us was by *fulfilling* the Old Covenant. That meant stepping in to uphold our end of the bargain, because we could not. And so God became one of us. He came to earth as a man, Jesus Christ, and lived a life that perfectly fulfilled God's standard, the Law. Then He, as a sinless man, offered to stand in our place and suffer the death we deserved for our sin.

One of the spiritual principles God revealed in the Old Covenant is that a blood sacrifice is required in order for *atonement*—repentance by the sinner and forgiveness from God—to take place: "For the life of the flesh is in the blood, and I have given it to you upon the altar to make atonement for your souls; for it is the blood that makes atonement for the soul" (Leviticus 17:11). Hebrews echoes this principle: "Indeed, under the law almost everything is purified with blood, and without the shedding of blood there is no forgiveness of sins" (Hebrews 9:22 ESV). For this reason, the Law required the High Priest to come before the presence of God once a year on the Day of Atonement (Yom Kippur) with the blood of animals to atone for the sins of the nation. But Jesus Christ, our perfect High Priest, achieved eternal atonement for us by offering His own blood before the throne of God in heaven:

Christ did not enter a sanctuary made with human hands that was only a copy of the true one; he entered heaven itself, now to appear for us in God's presence. Nor did he enter heaven to offer himself again and again, the way the high priest enters the Most Holy Place every year with blood that is not his own. Otherwise Christ would have had to suffer many times since the creation of the world. But he has appeared once for all at the culmination of the ages to do away with sin by the sacrifice of himself. —Hebrews 9:24-26 NIV

The Hebrew word for atonement, *kippur*, means "covering."[6] Jesus' atoning blood fully covered our sin, doing away with it once and for all. At the same time, His blood removed the spiritual "veil" that separated us from God, making the way for our communion with Him to be restored.[7,8]

After pouring out His blood and enduring not only physical death, but also the agony of spiritual death,[9] Jesus completely defeated sin and death when God raised Him from the dead. If Jesus had stayed in the tomb, Paul tells us, we would still be in our sins.[10] Instead, the resurrection life that brought Jesus out of the tomb is now imparted to us as we put our faith in Him, just as Jesus promised in John 3:16: "For God so loved the world that He gave His only begotten Son, that whoever believes in Him should not perish but have everlasting life."

---

[6] See Strong's H3725

[7] Then, behold, the veil of the temple was torn in two from top to bottom; and the earth quaked, and the rocks were split… – Matthew 27:51

[8] Therefore, brethren, having boldness to enter the Holiest by the blood of Jesus, by a new and living way which He consecrated for us, through the veil, that is, His flesh, and having a High Priest over the house of God, let us draw near with a true heart in full assurance of faith, having our hearts sprinkled from an evil conscience and our bodies washed with pure water. – Hebrews 10:19-22

[9] And about the ninth hour Jesus cried out with a loud voice, saying, "Eli, Eli, lama sabachthani?" that is, "My God, My God, why have You forsaken Me?" – Matthew 27:46

[10] And if Christ is not risen, your faith is futile; you are still in your sins! – 1 Corinthians 15:17

Now think about this. If *death* is spiritual separation from God, then what must "everlasting *life*" be? Life is spiritual connection with God! When you hear the term "eternal life," you shouldn't just be imagining a life in the future after you die and go to heaven. Eternal life is something we have and experience *now* through the restored Spirit-to-spirit relationship Jesus established with us through His death and resurrection. As we put our faith in Jesus, hand our lives over to Him, and learn to walk in relationship with Him, His eternal, powerful, supernatural, divine life becomes our life.

Our life for His life—this is the "great exchange" we must make in order to enter the Spirit-filled Christian life. Paul expressed it this way: "I have been crucified with Christ; it is no longer I who live, but Christ lives in me; and the life which I now live in the flesh I live by faith in the Son of God, who loved me and gave Himself for me" (Galatians 2:20).

Before we journey on and discover more about this exchanged, Christ-filled, Spirit-filled life in the coming chapters, I want to address some common questions that come up about the gospel.

But I'm a Good Person...

When people hear the gospel message, they commonly have one of two responses.

Some say, "But I'm a good person. Sure, I'm not perfect, but who is? It's not like I'm out there doing horrible things. Am I so bad that I need to be saved?"

You might not be so bad, *but your sin is*. God loves sinners, but He hates sin. To personalize it: He loves you, but He can't stand that darn sin that keeps trying to claw its way back into your life. This is what true love looks like! When you see someone you love doing something destructive, you hate what they are doing *because* you love them. The Psalmist reflected that

11

God has always been, "God-Who-Forgives, though [He] took vengeance on their deeds" (Psalm 99:8). God has a legal obligation to punish your sins, but a heart motivation to forgive you because you are His child. God is willing to separate you from your actions because He knows that is the pathway to change. He is willing to see you apart from your sin: to take vengeance on your sin, while forgiving *you*.

It might be easier to think of sin like a disease or genetic defect you couldn't help inheriting. If your doctor ran some tests and announced that you have a congenital heart problem that will kill you if left untreated, but then explained that a 100% effective treatment is available, what would you do? Even if you weren't feeling sick, wouldn't you pursue treatment to be safe rather than sorry?

In the same way, when the gospel tells you that the fatal disease of sin will destroy your life if left untreated, but a totally effective cure for sin is available to you through God's Son, the intelligent choice is to take the cure. The only catch is that you have to let the Holy Spirit treat the heart problem of sin in your life instead of trying to deal with it on your own. This is the paradox: The harder you try *not* to sin, the more tempted you will be to sin. If you try to "fix yourself" on your own, without God's help, you will only end up tired and broken. He is the only One who can transform you from the inside out. God is not after behavior modification; He is after heart transformation. (Heart transformation is the only thing that produces lasting change in behavior!) So invite the Holy Spirit into your heart, and let Him do the heavy lifting.

The cross of Jesus Christ separates you from your sin. While you may be a great person, none of us is good enough to meet God's standard. Romans 3:23 breaks the news that "…all have sinned and fall short of the glory of God." All of us were born spiritually separated from God, and cannot hope to live as He designed us in that state.

The Bible tells us that when we die, we will all stand before God and face judgment.[11] Before we die, we have to make a choice: will we be judged by the Law, or by grace? Another way to put it is this: will we trust in our own works or Jesus' works to qualify us as righteous before God?

If we choose to be judged by the Law, we must uphold each and every commandment outlined in the Old Testament in order to be deemed righteous. Even if we almost make it, but sin in one area of our life—*one single time*—the Bible says that's not good enough: "For whoever shall keep the whole law, and yet stumble in one point, he is guilty of all" (James 2:10). The Law requires a lifetime of perfection, and guess what? Perfection is impossible. Jesus Christ was the only man who lived a sinless life. The rest of us fall short.

We can't argue we're a good person, roll the dice, and expect God to pat us on the back and give us a gold star for trying really hard in life. If we're not perfect, we're imperfect. This is not a sliding scale; it is a choice of two distinct, opposing outcomes. When we die, we're not going to be compared to a homicidal maniac—we're going to be compared to Jesus Christ. So, unless our behavior can stack up to His (spoiler: it can't), choosing to rely on our own moral efforts and judgment under the Law will only leave us destined for eternal punishment.

Now that might seem a little unfair on the surface. Am I really telling you that even if you try your best, live a decent life, and give some money to charity, you can still end up in hell? Yes, that is exactly what I'm telling you! Heaven is eternity in God's presence; hell is eternity outside it. God cannot allow sin in His presence. If He did, He would not be holy. There's only one way for sinners to enter into God's presence, and that is by grace.

---

[11] And as it is appointed for men to die once, but after this the judgment... – Hebrews 9:27

Grace is unmerited favor. By definition, you can never earn or deserve it. Grace is a free gift you receive, simply by believing that Jesus took what you deserved and gave you access to what He deserves—full acceptance and approval by God. When you put your faith in Jesus Christ and believe that He took your place on the cross, you are forgiven and restored to right relationship with God (this is what "righteousness" means). With this relationship restored, you can live out the rest of your life in communion with God, knowing that He loves and favors you just as He loves His Son, Jesus Christ.

You Don't Know What I've Done!

Other people who hear the gospel don't have to come to terms with their need for grace—they know all too well that they are broken and sinful. For those of us in this second category, it can be difficult to come to terms with the truth that the gospel is powerful enough to forgive and cleanse us of all sin.

Quite often, people tell me stories of some event or issue in their past that seems insurmountable and unforgiveable.

"I can't possibly be forgiven," they say. "You don't know what I've done."

"I don't need to know what you've done," I explain. "All I need to know is Jesus already knows every detail of *everything* you have done. He paid for it on the cross, and He forgives you. Jesus Christ says your sin is forgivable. So who is right about your sin—you or God?"

If you insist that your sin and mistakes are unforgiveable, you need to understand that you're denying God's Word, which declares, "If we confess our sins, He is faithful and just to forgive us our sins and to cleanse us from all unrighteousness" (1 John 1:9). You're actually saying that you've done something so monumental that the *most monumental* work in the history of mankind—Jesus Christ dying on the cross—has lost its power. You're saying *you* know better than *God*.

God does not show favoritism[12]—He doesn't forgive some people and not others. Forgiveness does not have an age limit. There is no "red zone" to categorize sin, where some types of sin are forgivable but others are just too much. The Bible does specify that certain types of sin are more damaging than others. For example, Paul tells us to "flee" from sexual sin because of its destructive nature.[13] Notice, however, that we are told to flee the *sin*—not the cross. We must always come back to the cross of Jesus Christ, for it is there—and only there—that we find forgiveness for all our sins: past, present, and future.

Now, you may have heard that the Bible speaks of "the unpardonable sin." Jesus did say, "...every sin and blasphemy will be forgiven men, but the blasphemy against the Spirit will not be forgiven men" (Matthew 12:31). What is blasphemy against the Spirit? In short, blaspheming the Spirit means denying the gospel. The Holy Spirit's job is to convict people of the truth that Jesus is God's Son and that He is the only Way to God. Those who blaspheme the Spirit are those who either renounce their faith (become apostate) or those who, to their dying day, refuse to believe in and surrender to Jesus.

I've had people come to my office and say, "I can't come back to church because I've committed the unpardonable sin." I then explain that the very fact that they're even the slightest bit concerned with having committed the unpardonable sin proves they haven't committed the unpardonable sin. In order to become apostate, there is a permanent turning from God that must take place. Your heart must become hard and callous,

---

[12] For there is no partiality with God. – Romans 2:11

[13] Flee sexual immorality. Every sin that a man does is outside the body, but he who commits sexual immorality sins against his own body. – 1 Corinthians 6:18

unable to discern sinful behavior from righteous,[14] and unable to respond to the conviction of the Holy Spirit. If you're asking for help, or even thinking about asking for help, there is hope for you. As long as you have breath in your lungs, there is always time to turn back to God.

The Father's Heart

Along with convicting us that we are sinners in need of grace, and that abundant grace and forgiveness are ours in Christ, the Holy Spirit convicts us of something even deeper that lies at the heart of the gospel message: our Heavenly Father's immense love for us and His longing for relationship with us. Many people have the perception that the gospel is merely about God agreeing to pardon sinners and let them into heaven: that we found a loophole into heaven through Jesus and now God has to let us in! But the Bible tells us God isn't just forgiving sinners; He's restoring and reconciling Himself with estranged sons and daughters.

One of the most powerful illustrations of the gospel is Jesus' story of the prodigal son. In the story, a son demands his inheritance from his father, moves to a faraway country, and lives a lifestyle of hedonism and sin. When he runs out of money, he sells himself as a servant to a man in that country. Finally, in poverty, hunger, and humiliation, he comes to his senses:

> But when he came to himself, he said, "How many of my father's hired servants have bread enough and to spare, and I perish with hunger! I will arise and go to my father, and will say to him, 'Father, I have sinned against heaven and before you, and I am no longer

---

[14] And even as they did not like to retain God in their knowledge, God gave them over to a debased mind, to do those things which are not fitting... – Romans 1:28

worthy to be called your son. Make me like one of your hired servants.'" And he arose and came to his father. But when he was still a great way off, his father saw him and had compassion, and ran and fell on his neck and kissed him. And the son said to him, "Father, I have sinned against heaven and in your sight, and am no longer worthy to be called your son." But the father said to his servants, "Bring out the best robe and put it on him, and put a ring on his hand and sandals on his feet. And bring the fatted calf here and kill it, and let us eat and be merry; for this my son was dead and is alive again; he was lost and is found." And they began to be merry. — Luke 15:17-24

If you have felt the weight of true conviction for your sin, you can perhaps relate to the prodigal son's feeling of unworthiness. The most this son hoped for was that his father might have mercy and let him try, through lifelong servitude, to make amends for how he had dishonored him. Instead, his father runs to him, embraces him as his long-lost son, restores his dignity and position in the household, and throws a huge party to celebrate his homecoming!

This is the gospel. When you take even one little step towards God, He *runs* to you. He clothes you in the righteousness only Jesus deserves, and seats you with Him in heavenly places.[15] He calls you His beloved son or daughter. He guarantees restoration of your life on earth, and eternal ecstasy and celebration with Him in heaven. God loves you so much!

The gospel invites us into a relationship with the Father in which the revelation of His love for us is constantly unfolding, transforming us, and drawing us deeper into the Spirit-filled

---

[15] "But God, who is rich in mercy, because of His great love with which He loved us, even when we were dead in trespasses, made us alive together with Christ (by grace you have been saved), and raised us up together, and made us sit together in the heavenly places in Christ Jesus, that in the ages to come He might show the exceeding riches of His grace in His kindness toward us in Christ Jesus." – Ephesians 2:4-7

life. In the coming pages, we will explore what a life transformed by the love of God looks like.

Recommended Resources

Greear, J.D. *The Gospel: Rediscovering the Power that Made Christianity Revolutionary.* Nashville: B&H, 2011.

CHAPTER 2

BAPTISMS

Then Peter said to them,
"Repent, and let every one of you be
baptized in the name of Jesus Christ
for the remission of sins; and you shall
receive the gift of the Holy Spirit."

Acts 2:38

The Bible lays out several steps you should take in responding to the good news of the gospel. The first steps are *confession* and *belief*: "...if you confess with your mouth the Lord Jesus and believe in your heart that God has raised Him from the dead, you will be saved" (Romans 10:9). A confession of belief in Jesus looks something like this:

> Father, I know I'm not perfect, but Your Son Jesus Christ is. I put my faith in Him as my Savior. I believe that He hung on the cross and died as punishment for my sins so that I wouldn't have to. I believe You raised Him from the dead so I could have eternal life through Him. I want a restored relationship with You, and I rely on Jesus Christ for it! Amen.

If you have not yet made a confession of faith in Jesus, I encourage you to pray that prayer out loud! If you have made a confession of faith, then you have stepped into salvation. From here, the steps you take are all steps to walk forward in this new reality.

When you read the New Testament, you'll find that two of the first things new believers were taught to do were to be 1) baptized in water and 2) baptized in the Holy Spirit. These two baptisms are separate and distinct experiences, but both are powerful and essential to your growth as a Christian.

Water Baptism

Water baptism is a public declaration of faith in Jesus Christ. It symbolizes your decision to die to your past sinful life, trust Jesus to make you right with God, and begin a new life in Him. Paul explained this in the book of Romans:

> *Or do you not know that as many of us as were baptized into Christ Jesus were baptized into His death? Therefore we were buried with Him through baptism into death, that just as Christ was raised from the dead by the glory of the Father, even so we also should walk in newness of life.* —Romans 6:4-5

The word "baptism" comes from the Greek word *baptizo*, which means "to immerse." [16] James Montgomery Boice explained the nuances of *baptizo* in an issue of Bible Study Magazine:

> The clearest example that shows the meaning of *baptizo* is a text from the Greek poet and physician Nicander, who lived about 200 B.C. It is a recipe for making pickles and is helpful because it uses both words. Nicander says that in order to make a pickle, the vegetable should first be "dipped" (*bapto*) into boiling water and then "baptized" (*baptizo*) in the vinegar solution. Both verbs concern the immersing of vegetables in a solution. But the first is temporary. The second, the act of baptizing the vegetable produces a permanent change.[17]

Water baptism is a declaration that you are fully identifying with the death and resurrection life of Jesus, with the expectation that these realities will *permanently change you*. You are inviting God to permeate every part of your life and fill your

---

[16] Strong's G907
[17] James Montgomery Boice, *Bible Study Magazine*, May 1989.

whole heart.[18] The idea that you would make a confession of faith, be baptized, and then go back to life as usual is misguided. Baptism is a sign of a transformed life.

Throughout history, different denominations and churches have adopted different ways of performing baptism. Some require you to be sprinkled with water, while others fully immerse you in water. At CityLight Church, we believe in baptism by full immersion, because it seems apparent to us that this is the biblical model.[19] Nowhere in Scripture is there an example of someone being sprinkled with water and calling it baptism. Just as a literal burial involves the entire body, our spiritual burial and resurrection should involve the entire body. So get ready to get wet!

At CityLight, we also do not practice infant baptism, again because we find no Scriptural precedent for this. Babies can be *dedicated* to God—we see men and women in the Bible do that with their infant children.[20] But there is no example in God's Word of a baby being baptized. Baptism is an individual act of personal faith and obedience to Jesus. A tiny human being who can't even control his bodily functions is certainly not in a state to make a conscious decision for Christ.

Jesus' Baptism

One of the most obvious reasons to get baptized in water is that it is not only an act of obedience to Jesus; it is imitating His example. Though Jesus did not need to be baptized as a sign of

---

[18] I will praise You with my whole heart… – Psalm 138:1a

[19] If you would like to investigate this further, feel free to look at the following examples: Philip baptizing an Ethiopian eunuch in Acts 8:26-39, Peter baptizing Cornelius' household in Acts 10:34-48, and Jesus commanding His disciples to baptize all nations in Matthew 28:18-20.

[20] Hannah dedicated Samuel in 1 Samuel 1. Jesus was also presented to the Lord in Luke 2. After the Exodus from Egypt, God required that all the firstborn males of Israel be dedicated to Him until the Levites stood in the gap to fulfill that requirement (see Exodus 13:15).

repentance from sin, He told John the Baptist to baptize Him in order "to fulfill all righteousness" (Matthew 3:15). Jesus was acting as a model for all those who would step into a restored relationship with the Father through Him. When He did so, something extraordinary took place:

> *Then Jesus came from Galilee to John at the Jordan to be baptized by [John the Baptist] . . . When He had been baptized, Jesus came up immediately from the water; and behold, the heavens were opened to Him, and He saw the Spirit of God descending like a dove and alighting upon Him. And suddenly a voice came from heaven, saying, "This is My beloved Son, in whom I am well pleased." —Matthew 3:13, 16-17*

As Jesus came up out the water, the Holy Spirit descended upon Him. From that moment on, Jesus was empowered for His earthly ministry. Before His baptism, Jesus did not perform a single miracle; but after He was baptized in water and the Holy Spirit, He performed *thirty-seven* miracles recorded in the four Gospels, and the Bible hints that these were just a fraction of what He did![21]

Jesus' baptism sets a precedent for a supernatural shift to take place when we are baptized. When we do baptisms at CityLight Church, we fully believe that when people come out of the water, they will see evidence that they have been freed from their past and brought into their new future as a son or daughter of God. I have seen individuals come up out of the water and know God has set them free from a lifestyle of addiction. When I got baptized, I cried like a baby, felt a release from spiritual bondage, and understood for the first time that I was called into full-time ministry. My life was completely changed!

---

[21] "And there are also many other things that Jesus did, which if they were written one by one, I suppose that even the world itself could not contain the books that would be written. Amen." – John 21:25

Does getting baptized mean you'll never sin again? No. It simply means that God has launched you on the journey of learning to walk in the new freedom and power that belong to you through your new identity in Christ. (In the next chapter, we'll look more at the process of *sanctification*, in which we unlearn old sinful habits and learn to think, speak, and act like Jesus.)

Before I was baptized, my older brother, Chris, said something that prepared me for life on the other side of baptism. He told me that as soon as I was baptized, I would go and do something that made me feel like I had to get baptized all over again. He was right. I went out and did something stupid, and I felt like my entire baptism—all the crying, all the laughing, and finally taking the plunge—was a wash. But as my brother urged me to remember in that moment, *it wasn't*. It still was significant. It still changed my life and brought a tangible increase in the anointing (the tangible presence of God's Holy Spirit) on my life, empowering me for my earthly ministry.

Now I meet people who tell me, "I was baptized years ago. But you don't know what I've done since then. I feel like I need to be baptized again."

Just because you *feel* like you have to be baptized again doesn't mean you have to be! What God says took place at your baptism trumps your current feelings or past mistakes. Is there any real harm in getting baptized again? Of course not. However, it is by no means necessary.

The enemy wants to convince you that that the gospel is powerless to truly save and transform you. The moment you stumble, Satan will be there to accuse you and try to get you to believe that your faith is a fraud. His sole job is to steal, kill, and destroy.[22] But Satan is a liar. Don't let him convince you that baptism doesn't mean anything. It means the death of the old

---

[22] "The thief does not come except to steal, and to kill, and to destroy." – John 10:10

you, and the birth of a new creation.[23] Even Satan knows that, which is why he works overtime to convince you otherwise.

If you haven't been baptized, I encourage you to go ahead and do it. Do it because Jesus did it. Do it because He commanded that all His disciples should follow in His footsteps:

> And Jesus came and spoke to them, saying, "All authority has been given to Me in heaven and on earth. Go therefore and make disciples of all the nations, baptizing them in the name of the Father and of the Son and of the Holy Spirit, teaching them to observe all things that I have commanded you; and lo, I am with you always, even to the end of the age." Amen. —Matthew 28:18-20

The Baptism In the Holy Spirit

As powerful and significant as water baptism is, there is another, even more powerful baptism for you to receive as a new believer: the baptism in the Holy Spirit.

You may ask, "But didn't I receive the Holy Spirit when I gave my life to Christ?" The answer is yes, of course you did. At the moment of salvation, God's Holy Spirit took up residence inside you.[24] However, in the same way the Holy Spirit came *upon* Jesus at His baptism to empower Him to fulfill His ministry, so do we need the Holy Spirit to come *upon* us to empower us to live the Christian life and demonstrate the reality of the gospel.

Before He ascended to heaven, Jesus told His disciples to wait in Jerusalem for the baptism in the Holy Spirit: "…you shall be baptized with the Holy Spirit not many days from now… you shall receive power when the Holy Spirit has come upon you;

---

[23] Therefore, if anyone is in Christ, he is a new creation; old things have passed away; behold, all things have become new. – 2 Corinthians 5:17

[24] 1 Corinthians 3:16, 1 Corinthians 6:19, 1 Corinthians 12:3, Ephesians 1:13-14, Ezekiel 36:27, 2 Timothy 1:14, Romans 8:9

and you shall be witnesses to Me in Jerusalem, and in all Judea and Samaria, and to the end of the earth" (Acts 1:5, 8). The disciples followed these instructions, and sure enough, ten days after Jesus ascended, the Holy Spirit fell on them:

> *When the Day of Pentecost had fully come, they were all with one accord in one place. And suddenly there came a sound from heaven, as of a rushing mighty wind, and it filled the whole house where they were sitting. Then there appeared to them divided tongues, as of fire, and one sat upon each of them. And they were all filled with the Holy Spirit and began to speak with other tongues, as the Spirit gave them utterance.*
> —*Acts 2:1-4*

When the Holy Spirit was poured out on the Day of Pentecost, had all the disciples already professed their faith in Jesus Christ? Yes. But was there still *more* God wanted them to have? Yes! Is water baptism mentioned anywhere in this passage? No. This outpouring of the Holy Spirit refers to a separate and distinct experience in which Jesus fully empowered His disciples by filling them with more of His Holy Spirit.

You might think of the difference between the indwelling Holy Spirit and the baptism in the Holy Spirit as the difference between a damp kitchen sponge and a soaking wet, fully saturated sponge. The constitution of the sponge does not change as more moisture is added. But the ability of that sponge to cleanse and to pour out water depends completely on its level of saturation. When you receive the baptism in the Holy Spirit, you become fully saturated in God's power, ready to pour out His presence wherever you go!

The baptism in the Holy Spirit is essential if we are to reach our potential in God. Because every believer has received the Holy Spirit, every believer has the *potential* to hear from God. Yet not everyone does. Every believer has the *potential* to live a

25

life in which God demonstrates His presence with signs, miracles, and wonders. Yet not everyone does. Baptism in the Holy Spirit is the experience that translates that *potential* into *power*. It intensifies and amplifies God's voice, and invites Him to influence all areas of your life with resurrection.

Before the Day of Pentecost, the apostles already had the potential to minister the gospel effectively, but when they received the "power from on high," they were filled to the point of overflow. God's Holy Spirit was now free to communicate with them, and work through them, to turn hearts to Christ.

Sadly, much of the church has neglected the baptism in the Holy Spirit for centuries. There are some who argue that the baptism in the Holy Spirit is not an experience separate and distinct from salvation. Some say that we receive all the Holy Spirit we will ever receive at the moment we come to faith in Jesus Christ. Yet I disagree—both because Scripture demonstrates that the baptism in the Holy Spirit is a further experience available to us beyond confession and water baptism, and because it seems apparent to me that many Christians are not reaching their spiritual potential. Countless Christians live as vessels in constant need of refilling, but never become so filled with power that they pour out to those around them. The only explanation that makes sense is that they have not received the baptism in the Holy Spirit.

Evidence of the Baptism

When the 120 disciples gathered in Jerusalem were baptized in the Holy Spirit, they "...began to speak with other tongues" (Acts 2:4). Speaking in tongues, which we will explore more fully in Chapter 7, simply means speaking in an unknown language through the power of the Holy Spirit. Tongues is the *evidence* of having been filled with the Holy Spirit, and the fulfillment of Jesus' promise in the Great Commission:

"And these signs will follow those who believe: In My name they will cast out demons; they will speak with new tongues…" —Mark 16:17

Whenever I pray for a new believer (or an old one!) to experience the baptism in the Holy Spirit, I look for tongues as evidence. It is the one consistent and recurring biblical demonstration we see when a disciple goes through the baptism experience in the Book of Acts.

However, it's worth noting whenever we pray for the baptism in the Holy Spirit that speaking in tongues is not technically the end goal. The baptism in the Holy Spirit—an empowering and infilling which allows you to live a life fully devoted to Christ—is the end goal. We should never pray just to speak in tongues; tongues is only evidence. You can't have the evidence without the experience, and if we focus too much on tongues, the purpose of our prayers will be lost. So, while absolutely necessary, tongues should never be our primary focus. Speaking in tongues should simply be the natural byproduct of the baptism experience.

Let's say it's time for my wife and me to buy a new flat-screen TV. Maybe we've been putting up with a low-resolution clunker for way too long, and we want to experience greater clarity. We want to see in high definition. So I head off to the store, and I find the perfect new TV. It's going to be nothing short of life-changing. I check out, the cashier hands me a receipt, and I head home happy.

What was the purpose of the trip? A receipt? Of course not. I'm not going to get home and tell my wife about the amazing receipt I went and picked up at the store. I'm going to tell her about the TV. The new TV—that which is required to see more clearly—was the goal of the trip. But do I still need the receipt? Of course. The receipt is proof that I bought the TV. Any time I need to talk with the store about my purchase in the future, I'm going to need that proof. The receipt is evidence of everything I've purchased.

Baptism in the Holy Spirit works the same way. Jesus Christ purchased a full, restored relationship with God for all of us on the cross. He promised the fullness of His Holy Spirit to all His disciples. Our evidence—our receipt—is speaking in tongues.

When you start speaking in tongues, the possibilities for growth are endless. When you pray in tongues, God speaks through you in a heavenly language. The Holy Spirit, the same Spirit who knows the deep things of God,[25] can pray any prayer much better than you can, because He has God's heart! You will always be up to speed on heaven's agenda, and that privilege never expires.

Have you ever spoken in tongues? If the answer is no, don't panic! All Paul had to do was lay his hands on the Ephesians (see Acts 19:1-6 in the next section) and they started speaking in tongues and prophesying. Speaking in tongues takes just one small step of faith, and from there, the possibilities are endless!

If you haven't spoken in tongues yet (the key word is *yet*!), it's not a criticism or a problem; it's an *invitation*. God wants you to experience so much more of Him! Won't you say yes to His offer?

How It Works

So how do you receive the baptism in the Holy Spirit? Typically, you can receive the baptism as you receive prayer from someone who has already experienced it for him or herself. We see the early church grow as Peter and John prayed for people to receive the Holy Spirit:

---

[25] But God has revealed them to us through His Spirit. For the Spirit searches all things, yes, the deep things of God. – 1 Corinthians 2:10

> *Now when the apostles who were at Jerusalem heard that Samaria had received the word of God, they sent Peter and John to them, who, when they had come down, prayed for them that they might receive the Holy Spirit. For as yet He had fallen upon none of them. They had only been baptized in the name of the Lord Jesus. Then they laid hands on them, and they received the Holy Spirit. — Acts 8:14-17*

The believers in Samaria already believed in Jesus Christ. They may have even been baptized in water. But they were missing the fullness of the Holy Spirit. Peter and John had to travel to them and lay hands on them before they were able to enjoy God's Holy Spirit to the fullest extent. Peter and John had already been filled with the Holy Spirit, and it took the laying on of hands to transfer the anointing they had received to the believers in Samaria.

In addition to Peter and John, we see Paul pray for new believers to be filled with the Holy Spirit:

> *And it happened, while Apollos was at Corinth, that Paul, having passed through the upper regions, came to Ephesus. And finding some disciples he said to them, "Did you receive the Holy Spirit when you believed?" So they said to him, "We have not so much as heard whether there is a Holy Spirit." And he said to them, "Into what then were you baptized?" So they said, "Into John's baptism." Then Paul said, "John indeed baptized with a baptism of repentance, saying to the people that they should believe on Him who would come after him, that is, on Christ Jesus." When they heard this, they were baptized in the name of the Lord Jesus. And when Paul had laid hands on them, the Holy Spirit came upon them, and they spoke with tongues and prophesied. — Acts 19:1-6*

In Ephesus, Paul encountered believers who had never even *heard* of the Holy Spirit. Paul led them to Christ, and then prayed for them with the laying on of hands. The result? They were filled with the Holy Spirit, spoke in tongues, and prophesied. These believers were rescued from a life of confusion and nominal Christianity, and introduced to the fullness of God's Holy Spirit.

Sometimes, however, the laying on of hands isn't even necessary. Nobody had to lay hands on the 120 disciples gathered in the upper room on the Day of Pentecost; the power of the Holy Spirit simply fell as they were praying together. Your baptism in the Holy Spirit may happen after a church service as a member of a ministry team prays for you. Or it might happen as you're sitting in your room alone, listening to worship music and crying out to God.

God is not a God of formula; He is a God of obedience. If you ask Him what your baptism experience is going to look like, He will show you in prayer! Then, all you have to do is walk out what you have already seen in your spirit.

I once prayed for a young woman to receive the baptism in the Holy Spirit during a Friday night service. I explained the Scriptural basis for baptism in the Holy Spirit to her, and told her exactly what was going to happen: I would pray and lay hands on her, she would receive the baptism in the Holy Spirit, and she would speak in tongues! However, in the middle of praying, I heard God say, "Don't tell her to speak in tongues. Tell her to go back to her seat." I was confused. I knew tongues would be the evidence of her baptism, so why would God tell me to skip the best part?

I stopped praying, and I obeyed what I felt God wanted me to do. I asked the woman to go back to her seat, and smiled as she turned around, somewhat confused at the abrupt end to my prayer. Sure enough, when I glanced over at her several minutes later, she was smiling, laughing, and praying in tongues! God knew exactly the format she needed to be baptized in His Holy Spirit. If I had pushed ahead and blindly relied on what had worked in the past, she might have been denied this amazing spiritual experience. It wasn't my right to rely on formula; it was my responsibility to exercise obedience, and watch God work it out!

The important thing to know and believe is that Jesus will not deny you His Holy Spirit if you ask for Him: "So I say to you, ask, and it will be given to you; seek, and you will find; knock, and it will be opened to you. For everyone who asks receives, and he who seeks finds, and to him who knocks it will be opened" (Luke 11:9-10). Better yet, Jesus goes on to promise that when we ask for more of His Holy Spirit, we will never receive a counterfeit:

> *If a son asks for bread from any father among you, will he give him a stone? Or if he asks for a fish, will he give him a serpent instead of a fish? Or if he asks for an egg, will he offer him a scorpion? If you then, being evil, know how to give good gifts to your children, how much more will your heavenly Father give the Holy Spirit to those who ask Him!* —Luke 11:11-13

If you ask for more of God's Holy Spirit, God will give you more. The devil cannot come in with a counterfeit and make you think you are filled with the Holy Spirit, when in fact you are filled with something else. God is faithful to deliver everything He has promised to you, and a greater relationship with His Holy Spirit is no exception!

Pray for the Baptism in the Holy Spirit

If you feel you've been living a powerless Christian life, then you need the baptism in the Holy Spirit. The Book of Acts is not just a collection of stories of what *might have been* available to Christians in the past; it shows what *is* available to you now as a believer in Jesus.

God wants to give you His Holy Spirit in the same measure He poured out on the early church. The baptism in the Holy

Spirit is not dependent on God's willingness to bless you with a greater measure of His Holy Spirit; it is simply dependent on your ability to receive more of what God wants you to have. The Holy Spirit is not up in heaven, debating whether or not you are a worthy recipient, and waiting for you to pray the right prayer with the right intensity so that He might finally descend into your life. He already occupies your body; now it is up to you to let Him fully into your life.

Ask God for the baptism in the Holy Spirit. There is a significant, marked difference in the lives of believers who have experienced that baptism from those who have not. I see it every day in the lives of our members, and I have seen it time and again in my own life. God is waiting and wanting to work miracles through your hands. It's time to let Him.

Recommended Resources

Hagin, K.E. *Baptism in the Holy Spirit.* Tulsa, OK: Faith Library Publications, 2003.

CHAPTER 3

SANCTIFICATION

*However, when He, the Spirit of truth,
has come, He will guide you into all
truth; for He will not speak on His
own authority, but whatever He hears
He will speak; and He will tell you
things to come.*

John 16:13

So many people think Christianity is focused on behavior modification. The reason Christianity has this reputation is that, unfortunately, many Christians mistakenly think of their faith primarily in terms of lists of dos and don'ts: DO go to church, read your Bible, give to the poor, and be kind and loving to others; DON'T drink, do drugs, or break any of the Ten Commandments.

This is not life-giving Christianity. The behavior-modification model of Christianity is completely upside down. It is based on a false understanding of how God created us and how He brings about transformation in our lives. We are human beings, not human doings. Our behavior flows from the complex set of beliefs, convictions, and desires at the core of our soul and spirit. Because we live from the inside out, true transformation can only come from the inside. This is precisely where, and why, we need the Holy Spirit's help.

Relational Identity

When the Holy Spirit descended upon Jesus at His baptism, He was accompanied by the Father's voice declaring Jesus' identity: "This is My beloved Son, in whom I am well pleased" (Matthew 3:17). The Scripture establishes *who Jesus is* before it shows us *what He does*. Similarly, when the Holy Spirit comes to dwell within us and baptizes us in His presence and power, His first goal is to lead us into an understanding of our new identity in Christ. His role is to teach us to carry ourselves as true sons and daughters who walk in unbroken, intimate relationship with the Father and look just like Jesus. That's what the Christian life is, after all—thinking, acting, speaking, and living like Jesus, in Jesus, and for Jesus!

The identity of a son or daughter is a *relational identity*. Who you are is entirely defined by the relationship you have with God. Therefore, you can only live out that identity by embracing the truth of that relationship. In Romans 8, Paul describes the Holy Spirit's role in leading you to start walking out your identity in relationship with the Father:

> *For as many as are led by the Spirit of God, these are sons of God. For you did not receive the spirit of bondage again to fear, but you received the Spirit of adoption by whom we cry out, "Abba, Father." The Spirit Himself bears witness with our spirit that we are children of God, and if children, then heirs—heirs of God and joint heirs with Christ... —Romans 8:14-17*

The Holy Spirit is the Spirit of adoption. He makes it real to you that you are no longer spiritually orphaned, cut off from the Father. You are now a fully qualified member of His family. You are just as much a son or daughter of God as Jesus Himself. This means that all the rights, privileges, and responsibilities of a true son or daughter are now yours. You are royalty! Jesus is seated at the right hand of the Father in heavenly places,[26] and guess

---

[26] Now this is the main point of the things we are saying: We have such a High Priest, who is seated at the right hand of the throne of the Majesty in the heavens... - Hebrews 8:1

where you are? You are seated in Him![27] There is nothing you can do to earn adoption by the Father and all that comes with it. Your new relationship to Him is a free gift He bestows on you. All you can do is believe it and receive it.

The access to God we now enjoy as adopted members of His family stands in complete contrast to the access His people had before Jesus went to the cross. Seeing this contrast should help us appreciate what we have!

Under the Old Covenant, the only person who had access to God's presence was the High Priest. Once a year, the High Priest would enter the Most Holy Place—the part of the tabernacle that housed God's manifest presence. The High Priest would tie a rope around his body, and wear bells on his robes. The rest of the priests would watch and wait. If the High Priest did *anything wrong* in God's presence, he would drop dead. This was the punishment for disrespecting the glory and holiness of God. The onlookers would know the High Priest was dead because the bells would stop ringing. They would then pull his body out of God's presence—into safety—using the rope tied around his body.

When Jesus died, all that changed. The veil that separated God's people from His presence was torn in two, from top to bottom.[28] We now have full, uninhibited access to the Father. In fact, Scripture tells us to, "...come boldly to the throne of grace" (Hebrews 4:16). Under our New Covenant with God, we don't have to be afraid in God's presence! We don't have to worry about saying the wrong thing when we come before Him in

---

[27] But God, who is rich in mercy, because of His great love with which He loved us, even when we were dead in trespasses, made us alive together with Christ (by grace you have been saved), and raised us up together, and made us sit together in the heavenly places in Christ Jesus, that in the ages to come He might show the exceeding riches of His grace in His kindness toward us in Christ Jesus. – Ephesians 2:4-7

[28] Then, behold, the veil of the temple was torn in two from top to bottom... – Matthew 27:51

prayer or doing the wrong thing as we faithfully serve Him. The presence of God is now the safest place for us to be.

In order to receive and enter the reality of this new relationship with the Father, Jesus says we need to become like little children—to be "born again." [29], [30] Think about the relationship you (hopefully) had with your mother as an infant. You were completely helpless and dependent upon her to care for your needs. She fed you, dressed you, changed your diapers, rocked you to sleep, and stayed close to you. Just as importantly, she also spent a lot of "face time" with you. As you looked into her loving eyes, saw her smile of delight, and heard her voice, you began to form a bond with her. You learned to respond by mirroring her smile and making sounds that imitated her voice. Your face-to-face connection with your mother laid the foundation for your identity. Before you could even speak a word, you knew, "You are my mother, and I am your child."

Starting your relationship with the Father is a very similar process. By putting your faith in Jesus to save you, you are taking a posture of complete and total dependence on Him, like a helpless infant. He wants you to learn to cry out to Him and let Him care for you in His infinitely wise and perfect way. Above all, He wants you to develop a face-to-face connection with Him, because this connection is where you experience your new identity in Him. As you gaze into the face of your Father, you begin to know and believe who you are to Him and who He is to you at a cellular level: "You are my Father. I am your son. I am your daughter. You call me by name. You love me. You delight in me. You see me and know me. You want to speak to me and connect with me."

---

[29] "Assuredly, I say to you, unless you are converted and become as little children, you will by no means enter the kingdom of heaven." – Matthew 18:3
[30] Jesus answered and said to him, "Most assuredly, I say to you, unless one is born again, he cannot see the kingdom of God." – John 3:3

Your face-to-face connection with God is the source of all transformation in your life. The Bible describes that process like this:

> *Now the Lord is the Spirit; and where the Spirit of the Lord is, there is liberty. But we all, with unveiled face, beholding as in a mirror the glory of the Lord, are being transformed into the same image from glory to glory, just as by the Spirit of the Lord.* — 2 Corinthians 3:17-18

Everything about you comes to look more and more like Jesus as you simply "behold" Him—learn to walk in relationship with Him and align your thinking and behavior with His.

Sadly, many Christians never make "beholding" the Lord the foundation of their Christian life. They get tricked into thinking that becoming like Jesus must be earned through striving. They think God couldn't really be inviting them into a position of favor and access as a son or daughter if they haven't done something to deserve it. As a result, they cut themselves off from the voice and power of the Holy Spirit in their lives, and true transformation can never occur. It is so important that we don't fall for this lie about how to become like Jesus. We must always allow God to work *through* us instead of trying to work *to* God.

Love and Forgiveness

The fact that transformation works from the inside out does not mean we should not pay attention to our actions and behavior. Like any good father, our heavenly Father absolutely cares about our behavior, and He gives us many clear pictures and descriptions of the behavior He expects from us—the clearest picture being the behavior of Jesus. However, when the Holy Spirit convicts us that our behavior does not match Christ's, we must learn to recognize it as a direct invitation to encounter God more deeply in that place of face-to-face intimacy. It is there that God can impart the heart and character of Jesus, which will produce Christ-like behavior.

Two Scriptural examples show us how this process is supposed to work in our lives. Both of these examples deal with what it means for us to receive the revelation of the Father's forgiveness. Being forgiven is one of the cornerstones of our new identity as His sons and daughters, but it is a reality we cannot comprehend all at once. We must experience an ongoing, unfolding revelation of what it means to be forgiven, and Jesus tells us how to "check in" on how much we've learned. He says that when we truly know how much God has forgiven us, it will show up in our behavior in two ways. First, we will demonstrate extravagant love, devotion, and worship to God. Second, we will freely and fully forgive anyone who has offended or hurt us in any way.

In Luke 7, we read of a sinful woman approaching Jesus while He is having dinner at the home of Simon, a Pharisee. She kneels before Him, weeping, then washes His feet with her tears, wipes them with her hair, and anoints them with expensive oil. As Simon watches Jesus allowing this woman to make such an intimate, emotional display, he concludes that Jesus must not be as spiritual as he previously thought: "This Man, if He were a prophet, would know who and what manner of woman this is who is touching Him, for she is a sinner" (Luke 7:19). Reading Simon's mind, Jesus explains that Simon is actually the one missing the point of this woman's story. Both Jesus and the woman know exactly how sinful she is, but they also know something Simon doesn't know: all her sin has been forgiven. Jesus says to him, "I tell you, her sins—and they are many— have been forgiven, so she has shown me much love. But a person who is forgiven little shows only little love" (Luke 7:47 NLT). When we truly receive forgiveness, we can't help but respond with extravagant gratitude, affection, devotion, and worship to Jesus. Our love for God will grow in proportion to our understanding of His forgiveness.

Receiving forgiveness should also lead us to forgive others. In Luke 18, Jesus' disciples ask Him how many times they should forgive a brother who has wronged them. In response, Jesus tells them a story about a servant who owes an impossibly huge debt and is on the verge of being sold with his family into slavery. Astonishingly, at the servant's plea for mercy, his master responds by forgiving the entire debt. But what does the servant do next? He finds a guy who owes him a few hundred bucks, puts him in a chokehold, and has him thrown in prison. When the master hears about it, he is *furious*. He rebukes the servant for not showing compassion and, "...[delivers] him to the torturers until he should pay all that was due to him" (Matthew 18:34). Then Jesus makes a pretty terrifying statement: "So My heavenly Father also will do to you if each of you, from his heart, does not forgive his brother his trespasses" (Matthew 18:35).

The implication of Jesus' parable is this: If we're struggling to forgive other people in our lives, it means we have not yet grasped that God has forgiven us. When we understand that our own sin is an impossible debt that condemns us to a life of bondage, and that God, because of His great compassion and mercy, has saved us from this fate, then there's only one response we can have when someone wrongs us: we forgive the person *from our hearts*.

So what should you do when you see that your love for Jesus isn't as extravagant and wholehearted as the woman at Simon's dinner party? Or that forgiving someone from your heart seems impossible? The answer is not to beat yourself up as a failed Christian. Instead, ask the Holy Spirit for a deeper revelation of the Father's love, compassion, and forgiveness towards you. Remember, you cannot give away what you have not first received. As 1 John 4:19 says, "We love Him because He first loved us." If you want to be able to give away more love and forgiveness, you need to receive them from the Source.

If I'm Saved, Why Do I Still Sin?

You may have noticed that Christians are not perfect. They still sin after putting their faith in Jesus and coming into a relationship with the Father. This raises a lot of questions. Some people question the power of the gospel, or even their own salvation: "I thought I was supposed to be a new creation (2 Corinthians 5:17)? I thought I was born again? I thought if I was in Christ, I wouldn't continue to sin (1 John 3:9)? Either I didn't get saved, or the gospel doesn't work." Others wonder why God isn't stopping them from messing up again: "If I'm supposed to look like Jesus, why doesn't God just make me perfect all at once?"

Let me first assure you that the existence of sin in your life does not change the truth that you are, indeed, a new creation in Christ, just as the Scripture says: "Therefore, if anyone is in Christ, he is a new creation; old things have passed away; behold, all things have become new" (2 Corinthians 5:17). Your spirit has been resurrected and reconnected to God. Remember, however, that you are not merely spirit—you are a spirit, with a soul, living in a body. Though your spirit is reborn, your soul (mind, will, and emotions) and body must be transformed in order to express the new-creation reality of your spirit. The Bible calls this transformation process *sanctification*.

Sanctification means to make holy. Guess who makes us holy? The Holy Spirit! Contrary to what we might expect, however, the Holy Spirit does not have a magic button that turns us overnight from broken-down sinners to mature saints who never have a sinful thought. He doesn't work that way.

Think of anyone who has mastered a high-level skill or discipline, such as a concert pianist. In order for someone to reach that level of mastery, years of daily practice are required under the supervision of a master teacher who can assure that the pianist is developing and using the proper technique. It takes years of practicing scales and exercises, tackling increasingly difficult pieces, and overcoming performance anxiety. By the time the player has become a concert pianist, she has trained her body and fingers to the point where it appears almost effortless to those in the audience.

The Holy Spirit is our master teacher. By the time He is through with us, being like Jesus will seem effortless. That is His sole purpose, and He is 100% committed to fulfilling it. In order to get us there, however, He needs to train us day in and day out in the fundamentals of Jesus' character.

One of the biggest ways the Holy Spirit trains us is by convicting us when our thoughts and actions do not align with Jesus. It's very important to understand the difference between the Holy Spirit's conviction and Satan's condemnation. When you sin, it is likely that you will experience both.

Here is how you can discern one from the other. The enemy comes with the voice of shame and accusation: "See! You are such a hypocrite. You said you'd never do that again and you just did. How can you even call yourself a Christian?"

But the Holy Spirit's conviction always reminds you of who (and Whose!) you really are: "Hey! You're a son/daughter of God. What you did is not who you are anymore. Remember who you are and remember that I am giving you the power to walk in freedom over this issue! I love you!"

The more you listen to the voice of the Holy Spirit when you mess up, the more the power of the gospel will become real to you. You will discover that God is truly not afraid of your sin. He has fully and freely forgiven you of every sin—past, present, and future. It doesn't matter how many times you fall. If you cry out to Him, He will be there to pick you up every time. But He doesn't only want to pick you up; He wants to teach you that sin is destructive and free you from it forever.

Before we learn to walk in the safety and love of the Holy Spirit, we are actually incapable of seeing the truth about our sin. It's just too intolerable for us to look at our own pride or lust or jealousy or gluttony very long, because we can't handle the shame and guilt. But as the Holy Spirit convicts us of our true identities and frees us from shame and guilt, we can begin to let Him shine His light on the issues that have beset us and robbed us for so long.

We can finally discover that our lust is a perversion of our deep desire for intimacy. Once we see this, the Holy Spirit can reveal that God created us to experience true intimacy with Him and in right relationships with others, and we can begin to let Him define our desires in a way that brings life, not bondage.

Or we might discover that our gluttony is a false comforter we have turned to in order to self-medicate a deep wound of the past. When we see this, the Holy Spirit can help us to forgive those who hurt us, break off the lies we have believed about ourselves, and invite Him, the true Comforter, to heal and restore our hearts.

The only way the Holy Spirit can transform us into mature sons and daughters is by taking us through this process of learning to understand sin and righteousness at the heart level, and receiving His healing, grace, and power to walk in increasing righteousness and freedom from sin.

Please understand me—I am *not* saying that sin is ever permissible. God hates sin and Jesus died to set us free from it. The Bible clearly teaches that as we serve Jesus, we will become more like Him. Living a lifestyle of sin, therefore, calls into question whether you are really a disciple of Christ. I am not one to focus overtly on sin, however, because the gospel's victory over sin is a greater reality. If you're in a dark room, the solution to your darkness problem is not cursing the darkness and engaging it in spiritual warfare. The way to illumination is simply to flip on the light!

Spiritual Disciplines

For hundreds of years, generations of believers have found that spiritual disciplines are useful tools that the Holy Spirit can use to help them "flip on the light."

For some people, the very term "discipline" calls to mind duty, rigid control, and striving. But if you ask a concert pianist about discipline, you are unlikely to hear those words come up. Though she will say that her daily regimen of practice absolutely is work, it is not something imposed upon her, but something she willingly chooses, because it enables her to do what she loves and lives to do. Her discipline is what gives her freedom of expression.

In the same way, the purpose of spiritual discipline is to enable us to grow in doing what we, as sons and daughters, are learning to love and live for above all else—maintaining our face-to-face connection with our Father. Disciplines are tools that help us to "change the channel" and turn our focus away from the many distractions of our lives in order to focus on and fill our hearts with the reality of God.

In Chapter 5, we will be looking at one of the most important spiritual disciplines more thoroughly: the study of Scripture. The Bible is one of the Holy Spirit's greatest tools in our lives. Paul told one of his spiritual sons, Timothy:

> ...the Holy Scriptures... are able to make you wise for salvation through faith in Christ Jesus. All Scripture is God-breathed and is useful for teaching, rebuking, correcting and training in righteousness, so that the servant of God may be thoroughly equipped for every good work. —2 Timothy 2:15-17

Other key spiritual disciplines include prayer, fasting, fellowship with other believers, worship, praise, thanksgiving, and acts of generosity.

One particular demonstration that involves worship, thanksgiving, and meditation is the act of Communion (also called the Lord's Supper, the Eucharist, or the Mass). It's called the Lord's Supper because Jesus Himself instituted it during the Passover meal He shared with His disciples before He went to the cross. It instantly became part of the early church's tradition, so that years later, we read Paul writing to the church in Corinth about how to celebrate it:

> *For I received from the Lord that which I also delivered to you: that the Lord Jesus on the same night in which He was betrayed took bread; and when He had given thanks, He broke it and said, "Take, eat; this is My body which is broken for you; do this in remembrance of Me." In the same manner He also took the cup after supper, saying, "This cup is the new covenant in My blood. This do, as often as you drink it, in remembrance of Me." For as often as you eat this bread and drink this cup, you proclaim the Lord's death till He comes. — 1 Corinthians 11:23-26*

Communion is an act of remembrance. It is a way of placing before our minds the reality that Jesus died for us and established the New Covenant relationship between us and God. The act of eating reminds us that we must actually invite Christ into us and allow Him to nourish and transform us.

Unfortunately, the church has been caught up in a long debate around Communion. Part of the church believes in transubstantiation: the belief that the bread and wine literally become Jesus' flesh and blood as you take them. Others maintain that the meal is merely symbolic. Still others prefer to leave it a mystery. After all, Jesus neither said, "This becomes

My body and blood," nor, "This is a symbol of My body and blood." He simply said, "This is My body. This is My blood." [31]

All churches take Communion slightly differently. Some churches hand out nifty, pre-packaged cups with grape juice and a wafer of bread. Some churches ask you to kneel so a priest can administer the bread and wine to you. Some churches invite you to use both hands and tear a chunk of bread from a full loaf and then dip it in grape juice.

More important than the Communion debate or the Communion method, however, is the posture of your mind and heart as you approach the Lord's Table. Is taking the bread and cup a meaningless ritual to you? Or are you truly remembering His sacrifice in a way that leads to thanksgiving and worship, and deepens your true, spirit-to-Spirit communion with Him? Are you willingly obeying Jesus' instruction to, "...proclaim [His] death until He comes"?

The Bible is clear that we should "examine" ourselves before we take Communion to be sure we are taking it in a worthy manner:

> *Therefore whoever eats this bread or drinks this cup of the Lord in an unworthy manner will be guilty of the body and blood of the Lord. But let a man examine himself, and so let him eat of the bread and drink of the cup. For he who eats and drinks in an unworthy manner eats and drinks judgment to himself, not discerning the Lord's body. For this reason many are weak and sick among you, and many sleep. — 1 Corinthians 11:27-30*

How do you know if you're taking Communion in a "worthy manner"? Some churches restrict Communion to

---

[31] And as they were eating, Jesus took bread, blessed and broke it, and gave it to the disciples and said, "Take, eat; this is My body." Then He took the cup, and gave thanks, and gave it to them, saying, "Drink from it, all of you. For this is My blood of the new covenant, which is shed for many for the remission of sins." – Matthew 26:26-28

members only. I think that's on par with trying to restrict the Holy Spirit to members only. Communion is available to every believer. If you've given your life to Christ, confessed Him as your Lord and Savior, and if you believe He was raised from the dead, you're ready.[32] If Communion means something to you, then take it. If it doesn't, then don't. The distinction between "worthy" and "unworthy" is defined by who Jesus is to you.

Delighting in Him

Consistently spending time praying, worshipping, and studying the Word of God is so important, as is celebrating the Lord's Supper and fellowshipping regularly with other believers. We reap what we sow. When we spend our days reading the tabloids and watching reality shows, our brain is going to digest that input and recycle it in the form of desire, both conscious and subconscious. When we spend our days focusing on God, however, His will becomes our own. We will find ourselves no longer lusting after sinful things that used to excite us, but instead longing for more of God's presence.

When we focus on Jesus, everything else starts to fade. When we focus on holiness, sin starts to lose its luster. When we focus on light, darkness becomes an invalid concern. Have you ever looked up into the sun on a summer day and then tried to focus your attention back on the ground? Your vision becomes blurred. Suddenly you can't see the earth because heaven has left such an impression on your field of vision. God wants our times of intimacy, communion, and worship with Him to have the same impact.

David wrote, "Delight yourself also in the Lord, and He shall give you the desires of your heart" (Psalm 37:4). This verse has been perverted and abused. It is not license to ask God for

---

[32] …that if you confess with your mouth the Lord Jesus and believe in your heart that God has raised Him from the dead, you will be saved. – Romans 10:9

whatever we want and expect Him to provide it for us. Please do not recite this verse after asking for a Ferrari, and then look out into your driveway and expect to see your new car. David is saying that when we make *God Himself* our desire, He will give Himself to us. When we yearn for the presence of the Holy Spirit, He will make Himself known. We can't delight in God overnight, because transformation is a process. However, as we learn to desire God like an arid desert craves water,[33] He will satisfy us with more of His love than we can ever comprehend.

Recommended Resources

Frangipane, F. *Holiness, Truth and the Presence of God: A Penetrating Study on the Human Heart and How God Prepares It for His Glory.* Cedar Rapids, IA: Arrow Publications, 1986.

Leiter, C. *Justification and Regeneration.* Hannibal, MO: Granted Ministries Press, 2009.

---

[33] I spread out my hands to You; my soul longs for You like a thirsty land. – Psalm 143:6

CHAPTER 4

TALKING WITH GOD

Surely the Lord God does nothing,
Unless He reveals His secret
to His servants the prophets.

Amos 3:7

When you attend a Spirit-filled or charismatic church, chances are high that you will hear someone say, "The Lord told me..." or "I heard the Spirit say..." If you have never had an experience in which you recognized that God was communicating with you, these phrases might raise a few questions: "Does God speak to people? Will God speak to me?" The answer is yes!

Remember, the entire trajectory of the gospel is restoring our spirit-to-Spirit, face-to-face relationship with God. Can you imagine a relationship with someone who never speaks or communicates with you? If you can, here's a news flash: it's not a real relationship. You may dream about being best friends with Bono, but if he doesn't even know your name, that fantasy is pure fiction. The same is true of a relationship with God. As crazy as it might seem, the most famous, most important Person in the universe wants a real relationship with you, and that involves *communication*.

Many people, both inside and outside of Christianity, find the belief that God speaks to people uncomfortable, largely because it has been frequently abused. People have used "God told me" as a stamp of approval for all kinds of crazy things. In response, some parts of the church have established traditions and doctrines that only allow certain "qualified" people to hear from God, or maintain that today God only speaks to us through the Bible. The only problem with these kinds of correctives is that they eventually break down as well. The "qualified" people, as well as the most learned Bible scholars, have all been wrong at some point. Fear of deception so often leads to more deception.

Whenever we see something being abused, the answer is not to throw it out entirely, but to learn how to use it properly. If we are confronted with a counterfeit, it does not mean there is no genuine article it is pretending to be—quite the opposite. Rather, we must learn to discern between the genuine and the counterfeit, between correct use and abuse. We must learn to distinguish the Lord's voice from other voices and recognize the many ways in which He speaks. We must also learn to interpret and respond to His communication correctly.

The process of learning to discern the Lord's voice, like any learning process, requires continual instruction, trial, error, correction, and reinforcement. Think again of the analogy of a newborn baby developing a relationship with his mother and learning to communicate with her. He first begins to recognize her voice as the sound he consistently hears when he is experiencing comfort. Gradually, he makes out subtle changes in tone and articulation and tries to imitate them. Through her constant repetition and encouragement, he learns to speak his first word, then a few words. Eventually, he can understand many words and respond with short sentences of his own. Throughout a baby's journey of language development, his mother is providing instruction and correction—not only to his vocabulary, grammar, and pronunciation, but also to his understanding and interpretation of the messages they are communicating to one another. He makes many mistakes on this journey, but he learns as much from his mistakes as he does from speaking correctly, because his mother is there to help him discern between what is correct and incorrect. Above all, he experiences the exhilaration of learning and deepening his connection with his mother as his ability to communicate grows.

When you are born again, the Holy Spirit comes into your life like a parent and begins to teach you how to communicate with Him. Accurately hearing from God takes practice, and the Holy Spirit will guide you in that task. He is Spirit, and He speaks in many ways: through the Bible, through dreams and visions, through people in His church, and so much more.[34] This chapter is not meant to be a thorough examination of the many shapes God's voice takes, but rather an introductory lesson on how to position yourself to hear from God more by relying on His Holy Spirit.

Before He went to the cross, Jesus described the communicative role of the Holy Spirit in our lives:

> *"I still have many things to say to you, but you cannot bear them now. However, when He, the Spirit of truth, has come, He will guide you into all truth; for He will not speak on His own authority, but whatever He hears He will speak; and He will tell you things to come. He will glorify Me, for He will take of what is Mine and declare it to you. All things that the Father has are Mine. Therefore I said that He will take of Mine and declare it to you." —John 16:12-15*

The Holy Spirit is specifically assigned to communicate to you what Jesus and the Father are saying, and to *guide you into all truth*. If you want to hear from God and be able to discern true from false, the Holy Spirit must be your guide.

A Listening Heart

In Scripture, we find there are at least two factors affecting one's ability to hear and communicate with God: 1) the state of

---

[34] Please see the suggested resources at the end of this chapter for works that thoroughly examine the many ways we hear from God.

one's heart, and 2) the way in which God chooses to reveal Himself. God's method of communication is His choice; but the state of your heart is *yours*.

In John 5, Jesus rebuked the Pharisees—those who knew the Scriptures better than anyone. He said, "You search the Scriptures, for in them you think you have eternal life; and these are they which testify of Me. But you are not willing to come to Me that you may have life" (John 5:39-40). In other words, Jesus was telling them, "You have built your entire lives around studying, interpreting, and attempting to follow the Scriptures, yet you have completely missed the whole point of what they're saying. They're all pointing to Me! If you had understood the Scriptures, you would have recognized me as the Messiah and run to me."

In Luke 24, just after He was raised from the dead, Jesus gave a similar rebuke to two of His disciples. He caught up with them on the road to Emmaus, just as they were discussing the unbelievable news they had heard earlier that day about Jesus' empty tomb. In this case, the disciples did not recognize Jesus because "their eyes were restrained" (Luke 24:16), but they invited Him into their conversation. He responded:

> *"O foolish ones, and slow of heart to believe in all that the prophets have spoken! Ought not the Christ to have suffered these things and to enter into His glory?" And beginning at Moses and all the Prophets, He expounded to them in all the Scriptures the things concerning Himself. —Luke 24:25-27*

Jesus gave the disciples what He had not given the Pharisees—a thorough explanation of what the Scriptures were all about and how they pointed to Him. Yet they still didn't recognize Him as the Christ. Only when they sat down for dinner together did they finally see Him for who He was:

Now it came to pass, as He sat at the table with them, that He took bread, blessed and broke it, and gave it to them. Then their eyes were opened and they knew Him; and He vanished from their sight. And they said to one another, "Did not our heart burn within us while He talked with us on the road, and while He opened the Scriptures to us?" — Luke 24:30-32

These two stories show us two kinds of hearts. The Pharisees' hard hearts made them reject Jesus even when He was standing directly in front of them. The disciples' soft hearts burned when they heard Jesus' voice, even when they couldn't recognize His form. The disciples, unlike the Pharisees, had *listening hearts*.

These stories also show us a God who may choose to speak to us in an obvious way, or in a way where our eyes are "restrained" and we don't immediately perceive that He's the One we're hearing. When He does the latter, it's not because He wants to *hide* from us; it's because He wants to increase our ability to listen and discern Him in other ways. As long as we maintain a listening posture, we can be sure an "Aha!" moment is coming when He will connect all the dots for us.

The Holy Spirit wants to give us listening hearts—hearts that are leaning in and ready to respond to God's voice. It is the listening heart that gives us *spiritual conductivity*. What does that mean? Spiritual conductivity is like electrical conductivity. As you may know, some types of matter are more conductive than others. When lightning falls from the sky, for example, the impact that burst of electricity has on the earth depends on the material it strikes. If lightning hits rock, dirt, or some type of solid ground, the impact will be largely absorbed. A few seconds later, it will be as though nothing happened at all. If lightning hits metal instead of dirt, however, that electricity will be channeled through a receptive surface and dispersed. Best of all, if lightning hits a type of metal known to be conductive, all the energy can be channeled for use on this earth.

The active, living Word of God is the most powerful force in the world. God spoke the worlds into being. And God has created us as sons and daughters who have the potential for His Word to be channeled through our lives to impact the world. The degree to which we channel that force, however, depends on our spiritual conductivity—the state of our hearts. The Pharisees, despite all their religious training, did not have spiritual conductivity. When Jesus, the living Word of God, stood before them, His words simply hit with the thud of lightning on dirt. But when others heard His voice with a listening heart, that force changed them, and changed the world through them.

The good news is that we can all increase in spiritual conductivity if we are willing to be *refined*—willing to let the Lord take us through His process so He can train our hearts to take on a permanent posture of listening.

The refining process for silver is an excellent metaphor for God's heart-refining process in our lives. It just so happens that silver is the most conductive metal in the world. (Copper is next on the list, and gold is third.) Silver conducts the most heat out of any metal, and it's also the best reflector of light. It is significant, then, that David used silver to describe the Lord's words:

> *The words of the LORD are pure words,*
> *Like silver tried in a furnace of earth,*
> *Purified seven times.* —*Psalm 12:6*

David also used silver to describe the quality of those who had passed through God's refining process:

> *For You, O God, have tested us;*
> *You have refined us as silver is refined.*
> —*Psalm 66:10*

So what does it take to turn raw silver ore into the precious metal we find in jewelry stores? The first step is to place the ore in a solution of nitric acid to break it down and remove the silver from the other minerals in the ore. The silver is removed in the form of a white powder called silver chloride. The remaining waste materials are separated from the silver chloride and discarded.

This part of the refining process is a picture of God *removing* mixture from our hearts—the parts of us that would compromise us and make us unresponsive to His voice. He immerses us in His presence and gradually breaks the bonds we have made with lies through wounding or sin, freeing our hearts from these impurities.

Step two of the silver refining process is to mix the silver chloride powder with sodium carbonate and heat it to 1,200 degrees Celsius in a special furnace. The heat causes a chemical reaction, and two substances are formed. The first substance is silver—a pure, reflective, conductive, and extremely valuable metal. The second substance is sodium chloride: table salt.

This part of the process is a picture of God *adding* strength, wisdom, discernment, and purity to our hearts. The only way for these qualities to take hold, however, is for God to let us pass through fire! "Fire" is any circumstance in which pressure requires you to listen and obey God. When you come through the fire, the result is exquisite. Like pure silver, you have become the perfect conductor for God's voice. But not only does the refining process make you pure; it also makes you salty! It gives you flavor. God calls us to be the salt and light of the world, and cautions us never to lose our saltiness.[35] We stay salty by constantly asking God to refine us, filter out our impurities, and keep our hearts ready to hear His voice.

---

[35] "You are the salt of the earth; but if the salt loses its flavor, how shall it be seasoned? It is then good for nothing but to be thrown out and trampled underfoot by men." – Matthew 5:1

The architect of the refining process is the silversmith. Before the Industrial Revolution, a silversmith would stir the silver mixture as it was heated. And you know what? The silversmith didn't stop stirring—the refining process didn't end—until the silversmith could *see his own reflection* in the metal. In the same manner, God's refining process won't end until He can see His reflection in us! He has called and chosen us to "be conformed to the image of His Son" (Romans 8:29), and as we take a listening posture before Him, we "are being transformed into the same image from glory to glory, just as by the Spirit of the Lord" (2 Corinthians 3:18). The Refiner of our hearts is completely set on making us exactly like Him and revealing Himself to the world through us.

Joseph

So what does this refining process look like in someone's life? Throughout the Bible, we find many occasions in which God showed up and gave a clear word to someone about his or her calling and purpose. Sometimes the word came in a vision, a dream, or an apparition of God Himself, while other times it came through a prophet or human messenger. However it came, it irrevocably set the recipient on a path toward the fulfillment of the word. And it was on that path that the refining process unfolded.

Let's take a brief look at the story of Joseph. God's word over Joseph's life came to him in two dreams. In both dreams, Joseph saw himself in a position of authority—a position so great that his whole family, including his parents, would be under him.[36]

---

[36] Then he dreamed still another dream and told it to his brothers, and said, "Look, I have dreamed another dream. And this time, the sun, the moon, and the eleven stars bowed down to me." So he told it to his father and his brothers; and his father rebuked him and said to him, "What is this dream that you have dreamed? Shall your mother and I and your brothers indeed come to bow down to the earth before you?" – Genesis 35:9-10

Little did he know that it would be *thirteen years* before he saw these dreams come to pass. In those thirteen years, Joseph was the exact opposite of a ruler—he was a slave and then a prisoner in Egypt. He endured the rejection and hatred of his brothers, the betrayal and false accusation of his employer, and the neglect of those he helped in prison.

Yet in slavery and prison, Joseph excelled and rose to the highest possible position of authority as an overseer. Everything he touched prospered and was blessed. And most importantly, he never stopped listening to God. He not only continued to believe in the dreams God had given him; he became skilled in interpreting God-dreams for others. Finally, the day came when the ruler of Egypt had two dreams, just like Joseph had had thirteen years before. In an incredible moment, Joseph interpreted Pharaoh's dreams, and Pharaoh fulfilled Joseph's dreams by making him second-in-command over all of Egypt.

In recounting Joseph's journey to the fulfillment of God's promises, Psalm 105:19 says, "Until the time that his word came to pass, the word of the Lord tested him." The word "tested" is the Hebrew *tsaraph*, which means to refine and prove true.[37] As Joseph endured slavery and prison, the word of God for his life was refining him, preparing him and proving him worthy of the position God would eventually entrust to him. Even when reality didn't line up with God's promises, Joseph kept God's word close to his heart and listened to it above the voice of his circumstances. And when the time came for that word to be fulfilled and Joseph to take his promised place of authority, God knew Joseph would continue to listen to His voice above all others as he ruled Egypt.

When God speaks to you about who you are and what He is calling you to do, understand that His word will test you before it is fulfilled. Testing is not a bad thing. Before putting an

---

[37] Strong's H6884

aircraft in commercial flight for the first time, for example, airlines test the vessel to make sure it's ready to fly. They test its weight-bearing capacity and its ability to perform under strenuous circumstances. Only after it passes these tests can it carry what it was designed to carry. God will do the same with us! We're designed to carry His Holy Spirit. We're designed to fly! Although God is good and does not *cause* adversity, He will certainly *use* our trials to increase our ability to hear from Him so we can carry His presence into every circumstance.

Faith is not built in times of ease; it is built in times of trial. The Holy Spirit tells us that when our reality doesn't line up with God's promises, our faith is actually the evidence of the things we don't yet see.[38] It does not take faith to believe in something that has already come to pass. It does, however, take great faith to look at a situation that seems beyond redemption and trust God for His will to be done.

When we hear from God, we must have faith in His word. When we don't see His word take immediate effect, we cannot be discouraged. We can't resign ourselves to questioning if we ever even heard from Him in the first place. We have to trust all the more in His promises.

In fact, when adversity comes, we should get excited. Why? Because we're being tested. We're being refined. God is making us into the image of His Son, Jesus Christ. He is proving to us that His word is true. And once His word takes shape, and reality lines up with His promise, we will have become those who can be trusted with even greater promises.

Establishing Expectation

As a pastor, I believe every member of our congregation should hear directly from God. You don't need me to hear from

---

[38] Now faith is the substance of things hoped for, the evidence of things not seen. – Hebrews 11:1

God *for you*; He will speak *to you* just as readily as He speaks to me. Ultimately, my job is to put myself out of a job! If you don't need me in order to hear from God, then we're on the right track.

When you believe you can hear from God, you will. God is not seated in heaven, waiting for a chance to speak to you. He is speaking constantly; it's up to you to make sure you are listening. It's up to you to allow Him to refine you into someone who is willing and able to hear His voice, primarily through worship, prayer, and studying the Scriptures. There is always Scripture that is relevant to whatever you're going through, but it's your job to find it and use it, trusting that the Holy Spirit will guide you into all understanding.

So expect to hear God's voice. Then, once He speaks to you, do what He says! So often, people come to me saying they are struggling to hear from the Lord. My first response is usually, "What have you done with everything He already told you?" Often, we're not hearing more because we haven't truly listened to the last thing He said to us. Maybe the Holy Spirit highlighted a verse of Scripture to you as you read. Maybe you had a dream a few years back but never followed through on it. Maybe a still, small voice told you to make a phone call, but you never had the conversation. If you feel like you're not hearing God, the first thing to do is to go back and do whatever He already told you. God will give you more information when you fully utilize that which He has already shown you.

Jesus explained that obedience—keeping His commandments—is what prepares us to encounter Him more:

> "He who has My commandments and keeps them, it is
> he who loves Me. And he who loves Me will be loved
> by My Father, and I will love him and manifest Myself
> to him." —John 14:21

If we keep God's commandments, He will make Himself manifest—real and tangible—to us. If we listen to prior instruction, He will give us more.

Recommended Resources

Deere, J. *Surprised by the Voice of God*. Grand Rapids, MI: Zondervan, 2010.

Hagin, K. *How You Can Be Led by the Spirit of God.* Tulsa: Faith Library Publications, 1989.

CHAPTER 5

HOW TO READ THE BIBLE

Your word I have hidden in my heart,
That I might not sin against You.

Psalm 119:11

As you have likely noticed, everything we have been exploring about the Spirit-filled life is based on Scripture. The Bible is the authoritative record of how God has revealed His nature and purpose in human history and how He invites us to know and interact with Him. Though written over centuries by many writers in several languages (originally Hebrew, Greek, and Aramaic) and multiple genres, the Bible contains a complete blueprint of the grand "story" in which we find ourselves as Spirit-filled sons and daughters of God.

The beauty of the Bible is that it is accessible to every believer at every stage of his or her relationship with Jesus. Many people have come to faith in Christ simply by reading Scripture, without any special Biblical education. Saint Augustine, for example, converted to Christianity after hearing a child chanting the simple words, "Take and read." He saw the Bible lying open nearby, read the words on the page, fell under the conviction of the Holy Spirit, and said a prayer surrendering his life to the Lord.

Every mature Christian will tell you that reading, studying, and meditating on the Scriptures form an essential part of their spiritual disciplines, and that the Holy Spirit continues to speak through the Bible to refresh and deepen their knowledge of Him and His truth. If we want to experience the fullness of the Spirit-filled life and relationship with God, we must pursue increasing knowledge and understanding of the Bible throughout our lifetimes.

It's All About Jesus

Jesus, our model of the Spirit-filled life, knew the Bible (the Old Testament at that time) inside and out, as evidenced by His frequent references to Scripture in the New Testament. Yet as we saw in the previous chapter, Jesus pointed out that it was quite possible to read the Scriptures and miss their true meaning. The whole purpose of the Scriptures, both Old and New Testament, is to reveal Jesus and invite you to follow Him. Thus, the most pertinent question you can ask God when reading Scripture is, "What does this text tell me about Jesus Christ, and how can it lead me closer to Him?" As you ask, God's Holy Spirit will illuminate His answer. The clearest sign that you truly understand what you're reading in the Bible is that it is leading you to follow Christ more and more. As long as your use of the Scriptures continues to deepen your faith in and relationship with Jesus, your understanding of the Scriptures will be boundless. The moment you stop seeing Jesus in the text, you will be reading and studying the Bible in the dark.

Bible scholars often point out that Jesus is "concealed" in the Old Testament, but "revealed" in the New Testament. In other words, though the name "Jesus Christ" never appears in the pages of the Old Testament, everything about the Old Testament serves to create a framework for understanding why God sent His Son to earth. Without the New Testament, however, the true significance of the Old Testament cannot be fully perceived. Seeing Jesus revealed in the New Testament is the key to unlocking the concealed treasures of the Old Testament.

Let's look at how this works by reading a passage from Levitical Law:

Now the Lord spoke to Moses, saying, "Speak to the children of Israel, saying: 'If a person sins unintentionally against any of the commandments of the Lord in anything which ought not to be done, and does any of them, if the anointed priest sins, bringing guilt on the people, then let him offer to the Lord for his sin which he has sinned a young bull without blemish as a sin offering. He shall bring the bull to the door of the tabernacle of meeting before the Lord, lay his hand on the bull's head, and kill the bull before the Lord. Then the anointed priest shall take some of the bull's blood and bring it to the tabernacle of meeting... He shall take from it all the fat of the bull as the sin offering. The fat that covers the entrails and all the fat which is on the entrails...and the priest shall burn them on the altar of the burnt offering. But the bull's hide and all its flesh, with its head and legs, its entrails and offal—the whole bull he shall carry outside the camp to a clean place, where the ashes are poured out, and burn it on wood with fire; where the ashes are poured out it shall be burned.'" —Leviticus 4:1-5, 8, 10-12

God is speaking to Moses about the sin offering. Under the Old Covenant, if you intentionally committed sin, you were cast out from the Israeli camp. Even if you committed sin unintentionally, atonement was required in the form of a sin offering. To make the sin offering, the priest had to kill a young bull and pour out its blood. Then he had to offer specific parts of the bull to God, each of which had spiritual significance.

First, God wanted all of the fat of the bull as an offering. Why the fat? Fat represents the finest portion: that which is above and beyond what the animal actually needs to survive. It represents richness and excess. There was no USDA Prime designation when Moses was alive. The best cut of meat was not the leanest, but rather the fattest. Fat provides flavor, and would rise as a sweet smelling aroma before God. God wants our best, not just the leftovers!

Next, God asks for the kidneys. Why the kidneys? Figuratively, the kidneys represent the innermost parts: the origin of emotion and affection. In some translations of the Bible, the kidneys are translated as the reins—the part of us God can use to steer our lives when given over fully to Him. God wants our insides. He wants our hearts, our love and devotion. He wants our innermost parts.

But what about the outside? Notice that God tells Moses to take the flesh—anything that constitutes the animal's appearance and external characteristics—and *get rid of it.* Moses was to take the animal's carcass outside the camp, away from God's presence, and burn it.

Hundreds of years before He would send Jesus to make atonement for sin once and for all, God revealed something important about what atonement for sin really meant. By stipulating that only the insides of the animal were to be offered, God was telling us that atonement for sin was not simply a matter of cleaning up the outside (behavior modification). He doesn't care if we "look holy"—He wants our insides! Only when our hearts belong to Him are we truly free from sin. Our flesh, our works, and our own self-effort have nothing to do with our salvation. We are saved by our acceptance of God's love for us—our internal posture towards God's Son, Jesus Christ. God has been preparing His people for that reality throughout human history.

When you look for Jesus Christ in every single word of the Bible, you will find Him. Once you find Him, it will be impossible to lose that perspective.

When I was a kid, we did a simple exercise in school to illustrate the importance of perception. My teacher showed us a picture of a candlestick that looked something like this:

If you're only looking for a candlestick, that will be all you see. However, when you look closely, you'll notice the silhouettes of two faces on either side of the picture. If you don't know to look for them, you may never see them. Once you notice they exist, however, it's impossible to look at that picture the same way again.

The same is true of discovering Jesus in the pages of Scripture. The goal of reading is not to memorize facts and figures, or to be able to show off at church by quoting Scripture for your believing friends. The ultimate goal of studying God's Word is always to see Jesus Christ illuminated in every word, sentence, and phrase. This enables us to move towards Him and build everything in our lives upon the foundation of His truth.

Strategies & Resources

The Bible calls the Holy Spirit our Teacher, Helper, and Guide. Before you sit down to read the Bible each day, take a few minutes to pray. Invite the Holy Spirit to lead you as you read and study the Scriptures.

A lot of people mistakenly equate being Spirit-led with having no plan. This couldn't be further from the truth. God is not a God without plans. He is a brilliant planner and strategist, and He loves to release effective strategies to us, including strategies for reading, studying, and responding to His Word. So if you've never read the Bible before, here are some helpful keys.

Start reading in the New Testament. John's Gospel is a good place to see the love of Jesus Christ explained. Then move on to Mark to get a concise summary of the events of Jesus' life. Next, move on to Matthew and Luke to fill in all the missing pieces of the puzzle. After that, read the Book of Acts to continue Luke's narrative and watch how the Holy Spirit moved in the lives of the first disciples and the early church. Then pray He'll move through you in much the same way.

Personally, I love to read through the entire Bible every year. I use a simple plan from a website[39] that gives me some Old Testament, some New Testament, a Psalm, and a Proverb, every day. I value the structure and order that comes with a yearly reading plan. When I sit down to read and study, I already know where I'm going to pick things up. I don't spend any time figuring out where to start; I just dive right in according to schedule. I'm also a writer, so I write Bible commentary as I read. If I'm reading a passage of Scripture and something stands out to me, I write it down.

However, my method will not work for everyone. As a full-time pastor, I get paid to read Scripture. I recognize not everyone has that luxury. So here are some other ideas in case you're looking for something new to try:

1. *Read the Bible straight through, cover to cover, at your own pace.* This might take a long time, but it's worth it. And hey, you read every other book like this, don't you? Finding the right Bible will help. I recommend *The New Spirit-Filled Life Bible* (Thomas Nelson) edited by Dr. Jack Hayford.

---

[39] http://oneyearbibleonline.com/

2. *Read one chapter from the Old Testament and one chapter from the New Testament every day.* God is perfectly holy, and perfectly loving. We often struggle to hold these different attributes together in our minds. Reading a bit of Old Testament and New Testament every day will help you keep perspective on the fullness of God.

3. *Take your time and go through one chapter per month.* If you like to take deep dives and really do your research, this method is for you. Grab a helpful Bible commentary, and you're ready to go!

4. Use the Billy Graham method: *Read five Psalms and a Proverb every day.* Billy Graham once said, "I used to read five psalms every day—that teaches me how to get along with God. Then I read a chapter of Proverbs every day and that teaches me how to get along with my fellow man."[40]

5. *Don't ignore online resources.* I frequently use BibleGateway.com if I want to look at multiple translations of a particular verse. I also rely on BibleStudyTools.com for Greek and Hebrew translations, as well as Bible commentary. Both websites are free to use. Just be careful not to stray too far from well-known resources. Anyone can build a website, but not everyone is committed to teaching sound doctrine.

6. *Study the Bible in a group.* Most of my study time is individual. However, Scripture reminds us that, "As iron sharpens iron, so a man sharpens the countenance of his friend" (Proverbs 27:17). There are people in your local church who can help you

---

[40] Grossman, C.L. "The Gospel of Billy Graham: Inclusion." *USA Today,* May 15, 2005: http://usatoday30.usatoday.com/news/religion/2005-05-15-graham-cover_x.htm, accessed April 18, 2016.

understand Scripture. Find a local Bible study, and get plugged in. No man is an island, and studying Scripture with a group of like-minded believers is invaluable.

Responding to Scripture

Regardless of how you choose to make your way through the Bible, I highly recommend memorizing Scripture. Reading Scripture will do very little unless you incorporate what you read into the way you live your life. Professional athletes rely on muscle memory: they practice the motions used in competition over and over again, until they can respond effortlessly. Scripture memorization works the same way. When we memorize Scripture *before* we need it, we respond so much better as things happen in real life. Imagine what your life would look like if, at every turn, you knew exactly what God's Word says about every single obstacle you face! Memorizing Scripture is the way to get there.

When my wife and I first launched the Healing Rooms[41] at our church, I found every single Bible verse I could about physical healing. I wrote them down on index cards, and I memorized them all. Now, whenever I go to pray for someone, I have that arsenal in my back pocket. I have a repertoire of hundreds of verses that remind me what God's word says about healing!

If you're no good at memorizing, don't give up! God has actually made provision to help you memorize His Word. Jeremiah prophesied of a time when, after the Holy Spirit was poured out on the Day of Pentecost, God's law would be written

---

[41] The International Association of Healing Rooms exists to bring healing back to the body of Christ. We train teams of volunteers to pray for people with physical ailments, trusting that God's Holy Spirit will work through us to heal the sick. For more information, visit http://healingrooms.com/

in our minds and on our hearts.[42] That time is now! You are filled with God's Holy Spirit,[43] and you have the mind of Christ![44] Ask God for help. The Holy Spirit will help you to memorize Scripture when you ask Him.

Scripture memorization is a fundamental precursor to powerful prayer. One of the best ways to pray is simply to recite Scripture *out loud*. Psalm 1:1-2 says, "Blessed is the man…[whose] delight is in the law of the Lord, and in His law he meditates day and night." "Meditate" is the Hebrew word *hagah*,[45] which means to utter or speak out loud. In other words, when we memorize and repeat God's word out loud, we will be blessed! All the Scripture in the world is useless if we don't use it; but all the power in the world is available when we do.

Memorization and Biblical meditation (repeating, "chewing" on, and praying the Bible) are also precursors to *doing* what the Bible says. When God commissioned Joshua to lead the Israelites into the Promised Land, He said, "This Book of the Law shall not depart from your mouth, but you shall meditate in it day and night, that you may observe to do according to all that is written in it. For then you will make your way prosperous, and then you will have good success" (Joshua 1:8). God is describing a progression: meditation in the Scripture is the key to obedience, and obedience is the key to success.

Jesus ended the Sermon on the Mount with a similar exhortation:

> *"Therefore whoever hears these sayings of Mine, and does them, I will liken him to a wise man who built his*

---

[42] But this is the covenant that I will make with the house of Israel after those days, says the LORD: I will put My law in their minds, and write it on their hearts; and I will be their God, and they shall be My people. – Jeremiah 31:33

[43] But if the Spirit of Him who raised Jesus from the dead dwells in you, He who raised Christ from the dead will also give life to your mortal bodies through His Spirit who dwells in you. – Romans 8:11

[44] …we have the mind of Christ. – 1 Corinthians 2:16b

[45] Strong's H1897

house on the rock: and the rain descended, the floods came, and the winds blew and beat on that house; and it did not fall, for it was founded on the rock. But everyone who hears these sayings of Mine, and does not do them, will be like a foolish man who built his house on the sand: and the rain descended, the floods came, and the winds blew and beat on that house; and it fell. And great was its fall." —Matthew 7:24-27

If you want to build your life on the Rock that cannot be moved by any storm, it's not enough just to hear the words of Scripture—you need to *do* them. And in order to do them, you need to know them inside and out.

Now Go Have Some Fun

When you find yourself at a point when you really enjoy studying Scripture every day, you will be blessed beyond measure. It isn't easy to get there; in fact, it takes a lot of practice. But God's Holy Spirit is here to help. Ask Him to motivate you to delight in His word!

Reading the Bible shouldn't be scary. It shouldn't be just one more thing on your daily to-do list. It shouldn't be something you have to get done before you can relax; instead, it should be that thing you *get to do* in order *to* relax. Proverbs 16:24 says, "Pleasant words are like a honeycomb, sweetness to the soul and health to the bones." Whose words can be more pleasant that God's?

The Bible is not just a compilation of things God achieved, the likes of which will never be seen again. The Bible is a template of everything God will do for and through us when we yield ourselves fully to Him. Whatever God did through Jesus Christ and His disciples, He can do through you. In fact, the Bible says we should expect to see God work through us for even greater works:

> *Most assuredly, I say to you, he who believes in Me,*
> *the works that I do he will do also; and greater works*
> *than these he will do, because I go to My Father. And*
> *whatever you ask in My name, that I will do, that the*
> *Father may be glorified in the Son. If you ask anything*
> *in My name, I will do it. – John 14:12-14*

The Holy Spirit never died or left after the Bible was completed. He is alive and well. God will use Him to work in your life, just as He works through the pages of Scripture, when you seek to honor Jesus Christ in everything you do.

Recommended Resources

Bruce, F. *The Canon of Scripture.* Downers Grove: IVP, 1988.

Hayford, J., ed. *The New Spirit-Filled Life Bible.* Nashville: Thomas Nelson, 2013.

BibleGateway.com

BibleStudyTools.com

IntelligentCharismatic.com

OneYearBible.com

CHAPTER 6

PRAYER

Rejoice always, pray without ceasing, in everything give thanks; for this is the will of God in Christ Jesus for you.

1 Thessalonians 5:16-18

For the Spirit-filled Christian, prayer is not something reserved for Sunday morning church service or daily devotion. The Bible tells us to "pray without ceasing" (1 Thessalonians 5:17). This doesn't mean we are to recite scripted prayers every second of the day. It means we are to have a continual posture of communication with God. Along with developing a "listening ear" that is always leaning into God's voice, we should be having an ongoing conversation with God throughout our day.

In His Sermon on the Mount, Jesus gave us some essential guidelines for establishing a lifestyle of unceasing prayer—the lifestyle He modeled. First, He said that we should pray in the "secret place":

> *"And when you pray, you shall not be like the hypocrites. For they love to pray standing in the synagogues and on the corners of the streets, that they may be seen by men. Assuredly, I say to you, they have their reward. But you, when you pray, go into your room, and when you have shut your door, pray to your Father who is in the secret place; and your Father who sees in secret will reward you openly." —Matthew 6:5-6*

Jesus was not condemning public prayer. The New Testament repeatedly affirms the importance of the body of

Christ coming together to pray. He was condemning prayer that appears to be directed at God, but is actually intended to gain human approval—prayer that pretends to be for one audience when it's really for another. In order to build a prayer life that is purely directed at God, we must do it in secret, for an audience of One. We must learn to bare our hearts before Him with no one else around. Then we will be able to pray authentic prayers when we get together with other believers.

Next, Jesus said that we weren't to pray with "vain repetitions":

> "And when you pray, do not use vain repetitions as the heathen do. For they think that they will be heard for their many words. Therefore do not be like them. For your Father knows the things you have need of before you ask Him." —Matthew 6:7-8

Jesus was saying that our prayers are not to be repetitive or manipulative. Prayer should never be about leveraging our efforts to get God to do something that doesn't line up with His will. Why? Because He is our loving Father, and He already knows what we need before we ask. He knows, and He cares.

This begs the question: If our heavenly Father already knows what we need, then why do we need to ask Him for it? The simple answer is that God will not meet our needs outside a real relationship with Him, and that requires the intimacy and vulnerability of exposing our longings and needs to Him.

This shouldn't be too hard to understand if we accept that God is our Father. As a father myself, I can't imagine a relationship with my son in which he would never ask me for anything. I want him to ask me for things! Every request is an invitation to strengthen our relationship. Whenever I respond to a request—even when the answer is "No" or "Not right now"—I am sending the message, "I'm your dad. I love you and I'm here for you." The same is true of our heavenly Father. We don't just need His good gifts; we need *Him* to be our Father. That is why Jesus told us over and over to ask, seek, and knock, believing that our Father wants to give us good things; especially the greatest gift of all—Himself:

> *"So I say to you, ask, and it will be given to you; seek, and you will find; knock, and it will be opened to you. For everyone who asks receives, and he who seeks finds, and to him who knocks it will be opened. If a son asks for bread from any father among you, will he give him a stone? Or if he asks for a fish, will he give him a serpent instead of a fish? Or if he asks for an egg, will he offer him a scorpion? If you then, being evil, know how to give good gifts to your children, how much more will your heavenly Father give the Holy Spirit to those who ask Him!"* —Luke 11:9-13

The Lord's Prayer

After instructing us to build our prayer lives in secret and without manipulation, Jesus gave us a very important *template* for how to pray—the Lord's Prayer:

> *"In this manner, therefore, pray:*
> *Our Father in heaven,*
> *Hallowed be Your name.*
> *Your kingdom come.*
> *Your will be done*
> *On earth as it is in heaven.*
> *Give us this day our daily bread.*
> *And forgive us our debts,*
> *As we forgive our debtors.*
> *And do not lead us into temptation,*
> *But deliver us from the evil one.*
> *For Yours is the kingdom*
> *and the power*
> *and the glory forever. Amen."*
> —Matthew 6:9-13

If you have ever been in a Christian church service with traditional liturgy, chances are high that you have heard or recited this prayer as part of the service. While there is much value in memorizing and praying the Lord's Prayer as written, there's a whole lot more to praying "in this manner." The Lord's Prayer is not a formula, but a model that shows us multiple dimensions in which we should approach God in prayer.

I won't take the time here to unpack every word and phrase of this prayer—entire books have been written for that purpose. But I will introduce you to some of the main elements of this prayer so you can see what belongs in your prayer life.

The Lord's Prayer begins and ends with statements of *worship*: "Our Father in heaven/Hallowed be Your name…For Yours is the kingdom and the power and the glory." Worship is expressing personal adoration and reverence for God. When we worship, we put God in His rightful place in our lives. This is what it means for His name to be "hallowed." His name stands for all that He is. Our prayer life should be filled with worship that acknowledges who our Father is and what He deserves— the first place of love, honor, and adoration.

The next two phrases in the Lord's Prayer form a *declaration*: "Your kingdom come. Your will be done on earth as it is in heaven." God's kingdom is not a geographical place; it is a heavenly order that comes to earth whenever His will is expressed. Our declarations play a key role in the kingdom coming and God's will being done in the earth. When we use our mouths to agree with and speak out what God is saying about any particular thing, spiritual power is released. Therefore, our prayers should be full of declarations that express the will of God.

"Give us this day our daily bread," is clearly a request or *petition*. Again, our Father wants us to come to Him to ask for what we need. The very fact that He tells us to ask for *daily* bread suggests that He doesn't expect a day to go by in which we do not ask Him to provide. The way we make our requests is important, however. Manipulation is out of bounds, and so is *worry*. Jesus had a lot to say about worry in the Sermon on the Mount. The bottom line is, *don't do it*. "Do not worry" is a command (Matthew 6:25, 31, 34)! Worry accomplishes nothing, and it is inappropriate for us to worry when we have a Father who rules the universe, loves us unconditionally beyond imagining, and is working all things together for our good. Our prayer life should be filled with worry-free petitions made from a place of confident expectation.

The next phrase in the Lord's Prayer has several dimensions: *confession, repentance,* and *intercession.* "Forgive us our debts, as we forgive our debtors" is an invitation for you to expose your heart to the Holy Spirit and allow Him to show you where you need to make things right in your relationship with Him and with others. Confession means agreeing with God about what you've done. Repentance means asking God to help you change from the inside out—to change the way you think and the way you behave. Intercession—going to God on behalf of someone else—comes in with forgiveness. Forgiveness is an act that says to the person who has done you wrong: "I will not be judge over you. I am handing you over to God, who judges righteously. As I do so, I remember that I deserve eternal punishment and depend on His mercy and forgiveness as surely as you do." The Lord's Prayer invites you to turn forgiveness into a prayer: both for yourself, and for those you need to forgive.

Yet another category of prayer we find in the Lord's Prayer is *spiritual warfare.* "And do not lead us into temptation/but deliver us from the evil one" does not imply that God tempts us,[46] but acknowledges that we need His protection and wisdom to resist the attacks of the enemy. One promise of Scripture you can memorize is 1 Corinthians 10:13: "No temptation has overtaken you except such as is common to man; but God is faithful, who will not allow you to be tempted beyond what you

---

[46] "Let no one say when he is tempted, 'I am tempted by God'; for God cannot be tempted by evil, nor does He Himself tempt anyone." – James 1:13

are able, but with the temptation will also make the way of escape, that you may be able to bear it." No matter the circumstance, you can be sure that if you go to God in prayer, He will show you the way through it.

As you can see, God wants our prayers to be much more than bringing our laundry list of needs and concerns to Him. In prayer, we are to worship, make declarations and requests, walk through confession and repentance, intercede on behalf of others, engage in spiritual warfare, and much more.

Levels of Prayer

Using the Lord's Prayer as a template for our prayer life doesn't necessitate that we pray every type of prayer whenever we pray. However, it does mean that we should never allow prayer to become one-dimensional. It's very easy to let our prayer life devolve into only asking God for the things we need (petition), while neglecting the other kinds of conversations we need to be having with God. As a rule of thumb, I make sure that whenever I pray, I touch on three different areas: petition, intercession, and devotion.[47]

While prayers of petition are often the most obvious prayers to pray, there is more to them than we may think. Two factors shape our petitions: 1) our level of vulnerability and humility to acknowledge our needs, and 2) our level of faith in God's character and faithfulness to answer. The truth is that we often confine our petitions to things we think are acceptable, respectable, and reasonable, either because we are uncomfortable confessing our deepest needs, weaknesses, and longings to God, or because we don't really believe that God will do the impossible on our behalf. But God wants our petitions to be fully vulnerable and full of outrageous faith.

---

[47] For more on this, a great read is *Prayer that Brings Revival* by David Yonggi Cho.

When we come before Him to ask for what we need, we should be like the Psalmist, who wrote, "All my longings lie open before you, Lord; my sighing is not hidden from you" (Psalm 38:9 NIV). We should also remember that He is the One "who is able to do exceedingly abundantly above all that we ask or think, according to the power that works in us" (Ephesians 3:20). That means that our craziest, riskiest, wildest prayer of faith barely registers on the scale of what our God can and will do for us! What kinds of petitions would you make to God if you really believed that?

Sadly, few of us really experience the fullness of this first level of prayer, much less pass it and move on to others. Intercession—an even more powerful level of prayer—is accessible when you take your eyes off yourself, and start praying for others. It may seem counterintuitive, but the less you focus on yourself, the more God will satisfy your every need. Do you need healing in your body? Lay hands on someone else, and pray for their healing. Whatever God wants to get to them has to pass through you!

Intercession also means praying for the kingdom of God to invade the world. We live in a fallen world, but our mandate is to take back territory in the name of Jesus. All of creation groans[48] for us to stand up and do our job as children of God: to pray fervently for our world to be restored.

The best part of prayer comes when you move past petition, and even intercession, and get to devotion. Devotion means praising God with your whole heart. This is where the fun really begins. Have you ever just spent hours praising God for His goodness? David does this all throughout the Psalms, and we see the fruit of it in his life. Devotion is the most refreshing, life-giving part of prayer; yet so few Christians ever really learn to spend time consistently there!

---

[48] For we know that the whole creation groans and labors with birth pangs together until now. – Romans 8:22

Preparation

Jesus' lifestyle of prayer was the powerhouse of His ministry. Throughout the Gospels, we see that Jesus often went off by Himself to pray:

> *Now in the morning, having risen a long while before daylight, He went out and departed to a solitary place; and there He prayed. —Mark 1:35*

> *And when He had sent the multitudes away, He went up on the mountain by Himself to pray. —Matthew 14:23*

> *Now it came to pass in those days that He went out to the mountain to pray and continued all night in prayer to God. —Luke 6:12*

Though we don't have transcripts of these prayer sessions, we do know how Jesus lived as a result. He lived as a Man on assignment. He didn't live in reaction to circumstance; He lived proactively, as one who always knew what was expected of Him and what to do. Jesus told His disciples, "Most assuredly, I say to you, the Son can do nothing of Himself, but what He sees the Father do; for whatever He does, the Son also does in like manner" (John 5:19). Where did He see what the Father was doing? In prayer. Whatever God showed Him, Jesus went out and did.

Jesus taught and expected His disciples to prepare themselves for every situation in prayer. In Matthew 17, for example, we read about a man who brought his son to the disciples to be healed, but they could not heal him. No matter how hard the disciples tried, and how earnestly they prayed, the boy's condition would not change. Finally, fed up and frustrated, they brought the boy to Jesus:

Then Jesus answered and said, "O faithless and perverse generation, how long shall I be with you? How long shall I bear with you? Bring him here to Me." And Jesus rebuked the demon, and it came out of him; and the child was cured from that very hour.

Then the disciples came to Jesus privately and said, "Why could we not cast it out?" So Jesus said to them, "Because of your unbelief; for assuredly, I say to you, if you have faith as a mustard seed, you will say to this mountain, 'Move from here to there,' and it will move; and nothing will be impossible for you. However, this kind does not go out except by prayer and fasting." —
Matthew 17:17-21

Jesus rebuked His disciples because they hadn't spent sufficient time with God *in advance* of an emergency to adequately deal with the emergency when it came up. Jesus was not saying that the disciples should have waited until this father brought his son to them to start praying and fasting. Can you imagine coming to church, asking for prayer for healing or deliverance after service, and having the pastor respond with, "Come back in a week after I have prayed and fasted"? Of course not! When we're in the middle of an emergency, we might not have time to pray and fast. Rather, Jesus was exhorting His disciples to take on a *lifestyle* of prayer and fasting. He was making clear to them that the reason He was always prepared to heal the sick, cleanse the lepers, raise the dead, and cast out demons, was because He prayed *in advance*. Because Jesus made time to hear from God every day, He was always prepared for whatever came His way.

All too often, we wait until we have a problem to pray. If we wake up sick, we pray to be healed. If we find ourselves unhappy at work, we pray for a promotion. If we find ourselves in immediate physical danger, we pray for protection. But as sons and daughters of God, led by His Spirit, we are called to live proactively, not reactively. We're not to wait until we're in the middle of a storm to cry out for God's help! We are to pray in advance and know what's coming.

I start every single day with prayer. I wake up early, grab a blank sheet of paper, and write the day's date at the top of the page. I turn my cell phone on silent, close my computer, and eliminate all distractions. Then, I wait. I wait for God to speak to me, and tell me what He wants my day to look like. Whatever He tells me, I record. By the end of my prayer time, that whole page is usually full. I have a list of people to call, text, and e-mail. God's Holy Spirit has reminded me what needs to take priority on that specific day. Whatever God shows me, I go out and do.

Make time to pray at the beginning of every day. Ask God what your day is going to look like, in advance. As you ask, He will show you. No matter what comes your way, you will be full of faith to exercise and declare God's will over every circumstance.

Authority

The trajectory of your prayer life should be continually directed towards two things: 1) deepening your intimacy with God, and 2) joining Him as a willing servant and partner in seeing His will done on earth. Prayer is not about getting God to agree with your agenda; it's about coming into agreement and participation with His agenda.

The amazing thing is that God's agenda is partnership! He is a good Father who desires His sons and daughters to become mature representatives of the "family business." He doesn't want us to stay in some kind of slavish immaturity where we need to ask Him what color socks we should put on in the morning. He wants to train us to think, speak, and act like He does so He can send us out with powerful assignments, fully backed by all of heaven. He wants to entrust us with His authority!

From the beginning of creation, God purposed mankind to be His delegated authority on earth. He created Adam and Eve in His image, breathed His Spirit into them, and commissioned them to multiply, fill, subdue, and have dominion over the earth.[49] He—the One who spoke the world into being—also gave them the unique power of speech and a creative role in defining creation with their words. We see this in Adam's assignment to name the animals:

> *Out of the ground the Lord God formed every beast of the field and every bird of the air, and brought them to Adam to see what he would call them. And whatever Adam called each living creature, that was its name.*
> *—Genesis 2:19*

God was telling Adam to follow in His footsteps! "I did it; now you do it!"

Unfortunately, of course, Adam and Eve's journey to fulfill God's commission as stewards of creation was thwarted when the enemy enticed them into disobedience and usurped their authority. The devil became the "ruler of this world" (John 12:31) and brought humanity under his tyranny of sin and death. He hijacked and perverted our creative abilities, leading us to use our words to curse and bring death rather than blessing and life. Only when Christ died on the cross was the devil finally deposed, thereby allowing us to change our allegiance back to God and come fully under His authority once more. And coming under His authority allows us to carry His authority!

---

[49] Then God blessed them, and God said to them, "Be fruitful and multiply; fill the earth and subdue it; have dominion over the fish of the sea, over the birds of the air, and over every living thing that moves on the earth." – Genesis 1:28

The ultimate purpose of the gospel is to restore humanity to our original position and purpose as God's appointed caretakers and rulers of creation. That plan is unfolding as the Last Adam, Jesus Christ, who has been given all power and authority in heaven and on earth, recruits and trains disciples, who train disciples, who train disciples, etc.—all the way through the ages to you and me!

In a coming chapter, we will explore more of what Christ has authorized us to do as His disciples. But understanding God's original design and purpose for us, and Christ's restoration of that purpose, is essential in order for us to appreciate how powerful our words can be and why Jesus wants us to build a prayer life in which we learn to say what He is saying. Jesus said that His words are "spirit" and "life" (John 6:63)—that is, His words actually release the power of the Holy Spirit. When we speak as we are taught and led by the Spirit, in full agreement with God's Word, we can also release the power of the Holy Spirit—the most powerful Person in the universe.

Does this all mean that we can simply pray for whatever we want, and expect it to be delivered into our hands? Of course not! Any truth can be abused, and televangelists have certainly had a field day with this one. We always need to align our requests with God's revealed will:

> Now this is the confidence that we have in Him, that if we ask anything **according to His will**, He hears us. And if we know that He hears us, whatever we ask, we know that we have the petitions that we have asked of Him. —1 John 5:14-15, emphasis added

If we want our prayers to be heard, we need to pray according to His will. Is it God's will for you to have a Ferrari just because you want one? Is driving 200mph going to help you win people to Christ? I don't think so. So I'm sorry: praying for a sports car doesn't mean God is going to drop one in your driveway. The power of our words comes from reciting God's will back to Him, not from inventing prayer requests for our own personal benefit.

Bad Words

Stewarding the power of your words not only means speaking the right words over your life—it also means *not* speaking the *wrong* words over your life. Wrong words are anything that lines up with the lies of the enemy instead of God's truth. For example, two common types destructive speech I hear nearly every day are 1) cursing and 2) doubting.

A curse, by definition, is an offensive word created to inflict harm on another person. This includes swear words as well as slandering and cruel speech (e.g., the average "troll" on the Internet). I've heard some Christians make the argument that we should be able to use curse words. In fact, they say, we should even be able to curse in prayer! God will see our hearts and forgive us, right? But I completely disagree. Jesus said, "Out of the abundance of the heart [the] mouth speaks" (Luke 6:45). If curses are coming out of our mouths, it's a sign that our hearts have a problem. James says the same thing: "With the tongue we praise our Lord and Father, and with it we curse human beings, who have been made in God's likeness. Out of the same mouth come praise and cursing. My brothers and sisters, this should not be. Can both fresh water and salt water flow from the same spring?" (James 3:9-11).

What we speak is what we will see in our lives. So if you speak the promises of God everywhere you go, His Word will come to pass in your life. If, on the other hand, you curse, you will see the fruit of that in your life.

> As he loved cursing, so let it come to him; as he did not delight in blessing, so let it be far from him. As he clothed himself with cursing as with his garment, so

let it enter his body like water, and like oil into his bones. Let it be to him like the garment which covers him, and for a belt with which he girds himself continually. —Psalm 109:17-19

When we curse, we construct a barrier that that keeps blessings far from us. When we surround ourselves with cursing, we might as well be drinking poison! When we curse all the time, we become cursed! So think twice next time you get cut off on the freeway. When we try to curse others, we actually curse ourselves.

Doubt can be just as damaging as cursing. Words of doubt can actually cancel the miraculous. Consider what the angel said to Zacharias when he showed up to announce that he and Elizabeth would have a son. Before Zacharias could respond, the angel knew what was in his heart—doubt and unbelief. So what did He do? He shut Zacharias' mouth!

> *"But behold, you will be mute and not able to speak until the day these things take place, because you did not believe my words which will be fulfilled in their own time." – Luke 1:20*

God knew that Zacharias could talk himself out of a miracle. Are there any promises God has made that you keep telling yourself are too good to be true? Are you talking yourself out of blessing in your own life by speaking words of doubt?

The most important ingredient in your prayer life is faith. Eloquence doesn't matter. What matters is that you are praying out of a relationship with the Father. When you know to Whom you are talking and what He says about you, the prayers you pray will transform the world around you:

> *"For assuredly, I say to you, whoever says to this mountain, 'Be removed and be cast into the sea,' and does not doubt in his heart, but believes that those*

86

things he says will be done, he will have whatever he says. Therefore I say to you, whatever things you ask when you pray, believe that you receive them, and you will have them." —Mark 11:23-24

Recommended Resources

Cho, D. *Prayer that Brings Revival.* Lake Mary: Charisma House, 2001.

CHAPTER 7

THE GIFTS OF THE HOLY SPIRIT

Pursue love, and desire spiritual gifts…

1 Corinthians 14:1

Flirst Corinthians 13 is one of the most popular and frequently quoted parts of the Bible. Most of us have heard this "Love Chapter" read at a wedding or two (or twenty!). While this is fitting, it's also important to understand the context for Paul's eloquent discourse on love. Paul is not referring specifically to marriage when he writes, "Love suffers long and is kind…" (1 Corinthians 13:4). He is talking about the gifts of the Holy Spirit and how they are to function in the body of Christ.[50]

Historically in many parts of the church, there has been significant controversy and trepidation around believers seeking and using the gifts of the Spirit, simply because they have been improperly understood and used. The gifts of the Spirit are given for one sole purpose: love. They are designed to express and impart God's love to people in order to strengthen, encourage, and bless them. As we learn about spiritual gifts, therefore, it is essential to keep this purpose in mind. The Holy Spirit wants to give us gifts because He loves us, and He wants to love others through us.

So what are the gifts of the Spirit? Paul lists them in 1 Corinthians 12:7-11:

---

[50] Paul's primary teaching on spiritual gifts and their function can be found in 1 Corinthians 12-14.

> *But the manifestation of the Spirit is given to each one for the profit of all: for to one is given the word of wisdom through the Spirit, to another the word of knowledge through the same Spirit, to another faith by the same Spirit, to another gifts of healings by the same Spirit, to another the working of miracles, to another prophecy, to another discerning of spirits, to another different kinds of tongues, to another the interpretation of tongues. But one and the same Spirit works all these things, distributing to each one individually as He wills.*

The Greek word for "gifts" in this passage is *charisma*, which means "grace or gifts denoting extraordinary powers…enabling [Christians] to serve the church of Christ, the reception of which is due to the power of divine grace operating on their souls by the Holy Spirit."[51] This is why we use the term "charismatic" to describe those churches who believe that the gifts of the Holy Spirit are still active today, and therefore seek and practice them.

In the next chapter, we'll dive into the subject of healing and miracles. In this chapter, I want to cover the basics of the gifts Paul spends the most time discussing in 1 Corinthians 12-14—tongues and prophecy.

The Gift of Tongues

The gift of tongues enables you to speak to God and "utter mysteries by the Spirit" (1 Corinthians 14:2 NIV) in a language you don't know and can't understand, in order to be "strengthened personally" (1 Corinthians 14:4 NLT).

As we learned in Chapter 2, the gift of tongues was the initial evidence of the baptism in the Holy Spirit when He fell on the disciples on the Day of Pentecost. In addition to confirming the baptism in the Holy Spirit, Paul explains in 1 Corinthians 14 that the gift of tongues has two purposes. First and primarily,

---

[51] Strong's G5486

tongues are a personal, private *prayer language*. Second, and with considerably more discretion, tongues are to be used in public ministry.

You Need a Prayer Language

Praying in tongues builds you up spiritually. "He who speaks in a tongue edifies himself" (1 Corinthians 14:4), Paul wrote. Jude described this when he exhorted, "But you, beloved, [you are] building yourselves up on your most holy faith, praying in the Holy Spirit..." (Jude 1:20). As you speak mysteries to God in the Spirit, your spirit is being strengthened.

Praying in tongues also allows your spirit to pray without being filtered by your conscious mind. As Paul says, "For if I pray in a tongue, my spirit prays, but my understanding is unfruitful" (1 Corinthians 14:14). When you pray in English, your mind has to understand the prayer. When you pray in tongues, that step is removed, giving you direct spirit-to-Spirit communication with God.

There are certain issues in life that God will give us the ability to understand. However, every Christian will come across some issues that cannot be explained by human logic, reason, and understanding. In these circumstances, praying in tongues becomes extraordinarily useful. Tongues give us the ability to pray accurate, anointed prayers without having to understand what we're saying. The Holy Spirit knows exactly what we should be praying at all times. The Bible calls the Holy Spirit our Counselor and Teacher.[52] Partnering with Him to pray in tongues will often result in the breakthrough for which we have been waiting. If we want our prayers to line up with the

---

[52] But the Helper (Comforter, Advocate, Intercessor—Counselor, Strengthener, Standby), the Holy Spirit, whom the Father will send in My name [in My place, to represent Me and act on My behalf], He will teach you all things. And He will help you remember everything that I have told you. – John 14:26, AMP

Word and will of God, there is no more surefire way to make it happen than by praying in tongues.

Lest we think that praying without understanding (in tongues) is preferable, however, Paul exhorts us that praying *with* understanding (in English, or your primary language) is also essential: "What is the conclusion then? I will pray with the spirit, and I will also pray with the understanding" (1 Corinthians 14:15). Praying *without* understanding is essential for personal growth; praying *with* understanding is essential for testimony formation. When we pray with understanding, we know the requests we are making, and therefore know when our prayers have been answered. When Jesus called Lazarus forth and raised him from the dead, for example, He prayed with understanding so that everyone around Him could hear His petition to God and comprehend the power of effective, fervent prayer when God answered Him.[53]

Speaking in tongues should be so much more than something we just do when we run out of things to pray. Tongues should be an intentional discipline, and we should ask the Holy Spirit to direct us as to when we should be praying with understanding (in English), and when we should be praying without understanding (in tongues). I often start my daily prayer time in the morning by praying in tongues. As I pray, the Holy Spirit will give me direction (usually in the form of a vision) of what He wants me to pray for next. I then move from praying in tongues to praying in English, completely confident that I am praying what *God* wants me to pray for, as opposed to the first thing that is on *my* mind.

A Public Sign

The gift of tongues can also be used in public ministry as a

---

[53] And I know that You always hear Me, but because of the people who are standing by I said this, that they may believe that You sent Me. – John 11:42

sign of God's presence and power, specifically for those who do not yet know God: "Therefore tongues are for a sign, not to those who believe but to unbelievers..." (1 Corinthians 14:22a). In these instances, Paul instructs, the gift of tongues should always be accompanied by the gift of interpretation of tongues: "If anyone speaks in a tongue, let there be two or at the most three, each in turn, and let one interpret" (1 Corinthians 14:27). If an interpreter is not present, tongues should not be used publicly. Many newcomers to church have been turned off from God because they walked into a church service where one or more people were speaking, singing, or even shouting in tongues, and no one bothered to interpret the message for them so they could understand what was happening. This is a clear violation of the Holy Spirit etiquette Paul outlines in 1 Corinthians 14.

Receiving the Gift of Tongues

The Bible says we're supposed to *ask* for the ability to speak in tongues. When we ask, knowing that our request lines up with God's will, Scripture reassures us that we will have what we requested.[54] God promises us that when we ask for more of His Holy Spirit, we will get it. He also promises us that when we ask for the ability to speak in tongues, we will not receive a counterfeit.[55]

When you ask to receive the baptism in the Holy Spirit, the desire to speak in tongues is something you must cultivate. The decision to open your mouth and let God articulate heavenly

---

[54] "Now this is the confidence that we have in Him, that if we ask anything according to His will, He hears us. And if we know that He hears us, whatever we ask, we know that we have the petitions that we have asked of Him." – 1 John 5:14-15

[55] "If you then, being evil, know how to give good gifts to your children, how much more will your heavenly Father give the Holy Spirit to those who ask Him!" – Luke 11:13

sounds through you is a conscious choice; what exactly is *spoken*, however, is up to the Holy Spirit. Don't be surprised or concerned because you don't know exactly what you're saying. It is only by *surpassing* our understanding (which is different from simply *avoiding* it) that the Holy Spirit is able to pray superior prayers through us.

This is where trust comes into play. We must trust God, and we must trust His Word. The enemy will always try to invade our prayer time and convince us we're speaking gibberish and nonsense. He will try to convince us that we are making up sounds and phrases that have no meaning or significance to anyone. After all, why can't we understand what we're praying? How do we know we're not just going crazy?

It's in times like those that we must confess *out loud* that we know exactly what the enemy has come to do: to steal, kill, and destroy[56] our prayer life. Satan tries to rob us of our ability to communicate with God in tongues, kill off any revived intimacy with God that springs out of our ability to pray in tongues, and destroy any eternal fruit we're supposed to bear as a result of those prayers.

The reality, however, is that praying in tongues is extremely powerful. The whole reason for the outpouring of the Holy Spirit is to endow us with *power* so we can fulfill the Great Commission.[57] When that happens, Jesus' promise that we will do *greater* things than even He did will be fulfilled.[58] The enemy knows that, and will do everything he can to convince us that we do not deserve, or cannot obtain, the same anointing as Jesus

---

[56] "The thief does not come except to steal, and to kill, and to destroy." – John 10:10

[57] "Behold, I send the Promise of My Father upon you; but tarry in the city of Jerusalem until you are endued with power from on high." – Luke 24:49

[58] "Most assuredly, I say to you, he who believes in Me, the works that I do he will do also; and greater works than these he will do, because I go to My Father." – John 14:12

Christ Himself. It is our job to know and declare *out loud* that we can!

When you speak in tongues, there will be an intellectual hurdle to get over. You will immediately wonder, "Is this me talking? Or is this God?" The answer is *yes to both*. You are talking, in that you are making a conscious decision to open your mouth. God is talking through you, in that His Holy Spirit is determining what comes out of your mouth. You make a conscious decision to loose your tongue; the Holy Spirit makes the pointed determination as to how exactly your tongue moves.

Getting over that hurdle will be essential as you embrace and operate in other spiritual gifts God gives you. Let me give you an example. Some Sundays as I preach my sermon, I will receive words of knowledge for people, often in the form of a picture. One Sunday, I looked at a man in the sanctuary and saw a big, red apple hovering over his head. I felt a strong urge to approach that man and tell him, "God wants you to know that you are the apple of His eye.[59] He sees you and He still loves you, no matter what you've done."

In that moment, I could have convinced myself I was just making up the vision, and talked myself out of doing anything with the word God had given me. Instead, I stepped out in faith and told the man what I had heard and seen. Then the man told me his story. It turned out he had grown up in a Christian home, but had been living out his adult life in a pattern of addiction and abuse. That day was his first day back in church in many years. He had been fighting feelings of guilt and worthlessness for weeks; it had been the struggle of his life to come back at all. He left touched, with tears in his eyes, because I had heeded the message God was giving me and delivered it to the intended recipient. I made the conscious decision to look and see; God was the artist who painted the picture I would be able to share.

---

[59] Keep me as the apple of Your eye; hide me under the shadow of Your wings... – Psalm 17:8

Now we see why it is necessary to have the evidence of speaking in tongues if we are to move deeper into the things of God. If I remain convinced that God will not move my tongue and cause me to speak in languages I do not know, I will stay just as convinced that He will not give me words of knowledge, words of wisdom, or prophecies to pronounce over His people. If, on the other hand, I believe that He moves my tongue and gives me evidence that the Holy Spirit is speaking through me, it will be only a small step forward to believe that He is giving me other gifts of the Spirit. If I can't come to grips with the Biblical answer to "Is this me, or God?" as it relates to tongues, then that indecision becomes a conflict which will prevent me from hearing from the Holy Spirit in additional ways. However, once I have accepted tongues as evidence of baptism in the Holy Spirit, I have completed a faith exercise that will forever put my mind at ease as God speaks to me in new and greater ways.

The Gift of Prophecy

Paul spent a good deal of time teaching on the purpose and value of tongues—perhaps because it's the most mysterious of the spiritual gifts and can easily be neglected. He didn't want the church to miss out on this gift, which he himself used liberally: "I thank my God I speak with tongues *more* than you all…" (1 Corinthians 14:17, emphasis added). However, he did make it clear that when it came to corporate ministry, tongues were to take a back seat to another gift—the gift of prophecy:

> I wish you all spoke with tongues, but even more that you prophesied; for he who prophesies is greater than he who speaks with tongues, unless indeed he interprets, that the church may receive edification…Even so you, since you are zealous for spiritual gifts, let it be for the edification of the church that you seek to excel. —1 Corinthians 14: 5,12

The gift of prophecy is the ability to receive and declare supernatural insight and revelation from God. The Bible shows us that this revelation may come in a variety of forms—dreams, visions, signs, symbols, Scripture, angelic visitations, and even the Lord's audible voice. Paul urged the Corinthians to seek this gift above all: "Pursue love, and desire spiritual gifts, but especially that you may prophesy" (1 Corinthians 14:1). Paul valued prophecy so highly because of what it did for the church: "He who prophesies speaks edification and exhortation and comfort to men" (1 Corinthians 14:3).

There are a few important things to know about the gift of prophecy and how it functions in the life of a New Testament, Spirit-filled believer. First, the gift of prophecy is distinct from the "office" of a prophet. In Ephesians, Paul explains that Jesus has appointed people to certain offices in the body of Christ: "And He Himself gave some to be apostles, some prophets, some evangelists, and some pastors and teachers, for the equipping of the saints for the work of ministry, for the edifying of the body of Christ..." (Ephesians 4:11-12). As you can see, the purpose of these offices is to "equip the saints for the work of ministry." Far too often, believers get the idea that ministry belongs exclusively to the "professionals." That is not the New Testament model. The professionals are there to train and equip the *lay people* as ministers. If we're not doing that, we are not doing our job!

The primary role of the New Testament prophet is to give prophetic direction to the church and to train the people of God to use the gift of prophecy effectively. As with all the gifts of the Spirit, the gift of prophecy is not reserved for a select few. God invites *all* New Testament believers to operate in the gift of prophecy and live a prophetic lifestyle—and that includes you! It doesn't matter if you've never given a prophetic word in your life. If you pursue this gift, God will give it to you. He will speak to you in all kinds of ways so that you can boldly declare His word.

I use the term "New Testament prophet" because the Bible makes a distinction between how prophets and the gift of prophecy operated in the Old and New Testaments. In the Old Testament, only three categories of people could expect to hear from God: prophets, priests, and kings. Moreover, the Holy Spirit did not indwell these people as He does the New Testament believer. Instead, He fell or rested upon them on the occasions in which He wanted to deliver a word to His people.[60] However, one of the things God showed the Old Testament prophets was that a day was coming when His Spirit would not merely rest *upon*, but dwell *within*, God's people; and that this greatest of treasures would no longer belong only to a select few, but to all people:

> And it shall come to pass afterward
> That I will pour out My Spirit on all flesh;
> Your sons and your daughters shall prophesy,
> Your old men shall dream dreams,
> Your young men shall see visions. —Joel 2:28

Jesus announced this transition from the Old Testament prophetic paradigm to the New when He made this statement about John the Baptist:

> "For I say to you, among those born of women there is not a greater prophet than John the Baptist; but he who is least in the kingdom of God is greater than he." — Luke 7:28

What is it that makes the least in the kingdom a greater prophet than John the Baptist? It can only be the infilling and baptism in the Holy Spirit, which are the exclusive birthrights of every New

---

[60] "When they came there to the hill, there was a group of prophets to meet him; then the Spirit of God came upon him, and he prophesied among them." – 1 Samuel 10:10

Testament believer. If Old Testament prophets heard accurately from God because His Holy Spirit rested *on* them, how much more accurately should every New Testament believer hear God with His Holy Spirit residing *in* us! The same Holy Spirit who empowered Jesus for His prophetic ministry empowers *us* for ours! [61]

Another important point to understand about the gift of prophecy is its relationship to Scripture. Some people mistakenly think that when a New Testament believer speaks of "receiving a word from the Lord," he or she is claiming to be receiving revelation in addition to Scripture. This is absolutely not the case. Church doctrine and history affirms that the canon of Scripture has been complete and "closed" (admitting no additions) since the end of the fourth century. If you think God is "speaking to you," but what He's saying doesn't agree with Scripture, then the voice you're hearing is not God. God's spoken Word will never disagree with His written Word. Rather, the gift of prophecy helps us to understand and apply the Scriptures to our lives. Conversely, knowing the Scriptures helps us to test our prophetic words so we can make sure they align and harmonize with this foundational revelation from God.

Prophetic Etiquette

One of the main roles of the Old Testament prophets was to call God's people back to Him when they strayed away. For this reason, many of the Old Testament prophecies contain passionate calls to repentance and warnings of impending judgment should God's people continue in rebellion and sin.

---

[61] But if the Spirit of Him who raised Jesus from the dead dwells in you, He who raised Christ from the dead will also give life to your mortal bodies through His Spirit who dwells in you. – Romans 8:11

In the New Testament, the message of judgment and repentance is completely transformed and repositioned in the prophetic ministry to the church, for an obvious reason: those who belong to the kingdom of God are there because they *have* repented and acknowledged that the judgment they deserved was fully poured out on Christ! This is why the gift of prophecy is now directed towards giving "edification and exhortation and comfort" (1 Corinthians 14:3) to the church.

Obviously, the church is called to preach and proclaim the gospel to the world, which does include a call to repentance from sin. But we make this appeal by putting the goodness of God on display, for "the goodness of God leads [mankind] to repentance" (Romans 2:4). Instead of threatening people with fire and brimstone, we are called to display the loving heart of the Father who has sacrificed everything to call His lost sons and daughters home.

Remember, the ultimate goal when exercising any spiritual gift is love. The power of the gift of prophecy is seen most clearly as it affirms the Father's heart of love for His people. He alone can give us the supernatural ability to look at a person who is covered with shame and living in sin and call out their true identity as a beloved son or daughter. It's all too easy to see the dirt in people's lives. The Spirit gives us the ability to see the gold hidden under the dirt!

Believers can cause a lot of damage when they use spiritual gifts to call out the dirt instead of the gold. I once heard a troubling story from a member at a local church. She had gone up for prayer after service and asked for a member of the ministry team to pray for her. The first thing the minister said to her was, "You are struggling with a spirit of homosexuality." The woman left that encounter troubled and confused. She had struggled with homosexual thoughts about other women years before, but it hadn't happened for a long time. After the prayer, she went home and actually started *fearing* that homosexual desires might surface in her life. Instead of leaving the prayer session empowered and fearless, she left it powerless and fearful.

Did that man on the ministry team really hear from the Holy Spirit? It's possible. One of the gifts of the Spirit is the ability to discern spirits. However, discerning sin or demonic oppression in someone's life does not mean we are to automatically prophesy what we are seeing or hearing. Rather, we must ask the Holy Spirit for wisdom about what He wants us to do with this information, as well as asking Him for more insight: "Okay, I see some of the dirt. Will You show me the gold in this person's life? Who do You say they are? How do You feel about them? How do You want me to bring edification, exhortation, and comfort to them?"

Sometimes the Holy Spirit will tell you that you are simply to pray silently for that issue in the person's life. Occasionally, He may lead you to ask about it in a tactful way. For example, this man might have asked, "Do you have the desire to be married?" or even simply asked her if she had ever struggled with thoughts about other women, instead of making the presumptuous declaration that she had. He could have then proceeded to pray with sensitivity, based on her response. Most often, the Holy Spirit will give you *overwhelming compassion* for the person and show you how to pray and prophesy in the "opposite spirit." In this case, the man might have said, "God is going to make you confident in your romantic relationships," or "God is healing your identity and giving you His grace and anointing to walk in wholeness and purity." When we speak the positive in spite of the negative, we prophesy life instead of death.

In the Gospels, we find many examples of Jesus ministering prophetically to individuals in ways that called out the gold in them. One of the greatest examples is found in John 4, where Jesus ministers to a woman at a well in Samaria. Jesus didn't mince words or avoid addressing the woman's problems—He immediately called out some areas in her life that needed work. However, He presented His prophetic word with love. He treated her with such dignity and compassion that she ran into the city and shouted to all her friends, "Come, see a Man who told me all things that I ever did. Could this be the Christ?" (John 4:29). As a result, everyone she met "…went out of the city and came to Him" (John 4:30). A loving prophetic word draws people out of bondage and into freedom and life in Christ.

Sadly, Christians are well known for identifying the things we are *against* and asking others to change. We are much less known for calling out the things we are *for* and giving others grace to transform. Will you be part of a new generation of worshippers—intelligent Charismatics—who take the time to dig for the gold in people, even when all you can see is dirt?

Testing Prophetic Words

Because we live in a New Testament prophetic paradigm, it's important to remember that God's design and purpose is for every person, even someone who doesn't know Him yet, to be able to hear from God for him or herself. None of us is to replace the Holy Spirit in a person's life. For this reason, as a rule of thumb, we should avoid giving imperatives (i.e. commanding instructions) as prophetic words to other people.[62] Also, when we deliver a word, we should encourage the recipient to test the word. Scriptural soundness is the first litmus test of any prophetic word. The second is, does the person receiving the word agree? Does the word line up with what he or she is already hearing from God in times of personal prayer?

The person God will speak to most often about your life is *you*. We live in a culture where we have become overly reliant

---

[62] At CityLight Church, our "Don'ts" for prophetic words are: No mates, no dates, no correction, and no direction.

on help from experts. When it comes to prophecy, we often think we need to visit a prophetic conference or travel across the country to hear a guest minister to get our hands on what God is saying. That couldn't be further from the truth. Any prophetic word you receive should *confirm* what God is already speaking to you. If it doesn't, put it in your back pocket as a reference and move forward. With several supernatural exceptions, I have rarely seen God prophetically pronounce destiny over someone through another believer before He personally speaks to that person about his or her own destiny.

God spoke to me about becoming a pastor for *years* before I moved into full-time ministry. When I was growing up, our church hosted a "Youth Sunday" every year. As a senior in high school, I gave the sermon on Youth Sunday. After I was done speaking, a woman in the congregation stopped me at the back of the sanctuary. "Would you ever think about becoming a pastor?" she asked. I pulled a Sarah:[63] I laughed!

Over a decade later, as I felt the call to become a pastor coming into focus, my lead pastor gave me some great advice. He told me to make sure God confirmed my calling into full-time ministry through a trusted prophetic voice. In moments of doubt and weakness, he said, I would benefit from confident reliance on that prophetic word. God was already speaking to me in prayer about working at the church, and He had entrusted specific vision to me as to how my transition from the financial services industry into ministry would unfold. So, I asked God for confirmation from a trusted prophetic voice.

Several weeks later, my wife and I were at a Christian conference in upstate New York. Halfway through the program, one of the speakers stopped and said, "I feel like there is a couple here from New York City, and I am supposed to pray for them." How did he know we were there!? We had never met

---

[63] Therefore Sarah laughed within herself, saying, "After I have grown old, shall I have pleasure, my lord being old also?" – Genesis 18:12

him before, and he had no way of knowing where we were from.

As we walked to the stage, I felt my spirit leap within me. I felt tingling all over my body as God got ready to publicly pronounce His calling over my life. Once we were at the stage, the speaker simply said, "You are a pastor." I was undone. That was all I needed to hear! God had publicly confirmed the destiny He had been speaking to me for years in secret.

However, we must note the difference between *confirmation* of an existing idea, and the *introduction* of a brand-new idea. I have seen too many casualties from people in our churches being misled by a guest speaker who pronounces a destiny that doesn't agree with what they're hearing in personal prayer time. If God wants you to be a pastor, He will speak to *you* about being a pastor first. If it's time to get married, God will speak to *you* about your spouse. The person to whom God wants to communicate your destiny most is *you*!

As with any other spiritual gift, prophetic discretion is always wise. The spirit of the prophet is subject to the prophet.[64] In other words, God will rarely overwhelm you to the point of no control. Yes, there may be times when God's presence overpowers you so strongly that you break posture, fall to the ground, and roar with laughter (more on this in the next chapter). However, this will be the exception rather than the rule. We must share prophetic words with enthusiasm; but we must temper any unprofitable enthusiasm with discretion.[65] When we translate heaven's words so that non-believers can understand them, whole cities will be won for Jesus Christ.

Lastly, there is a difference between individual and corporate words. God will speak personal secrets to you for

---

[64] "And the spirits of the prophets are subject to the prophets. For God is not the author of confusion but of peace, as in all the churches of the saints." – 1 Corinthians 14:32-33

[65] "All things are lawful for me, but not all things are helpful; all things are lawful for me, but not all things edify." – 1 Corinthians 10:23

your own edification that are not necessarily meant to be shared with others. In Genesis 37, Joseph got into trouble because he shared his dreams of prosperity and power with his brothers. In the first dream, his brothers bowed down to him.[66] In the second dream, his parents and his brothers all submitted to his authority![67] Needless to say, Joseph should have kept these dreams to himself. Joseph confused personal prophetic dreams with corporate words that were to be shared; and he suffered the consequences of that confusion in captivity. God will speak amazing things to you, but not everything He shares should be spoken from a pulpit. Wisdom means knowing the difference between individual and corporate prophetic words.

How to Prophesy

Prophecy is serious business. Under the Old Covenant, any prophet who falsely reported the word of God could be stoned! Thank God we live under a New Covenant through Jesus Christ. God invites us to receive His word so that we can share it with other people. Freely we have received, and freely we must give!

First, spend time in the Bible. The purpose of the gift of prophecy is to speak God's word out over His people. You cannot speak what you do not know. Reading Scripture will also give you the chance to explore the lives and ministries of Old Testament prophets like Isaiah, Jeremiah, Ezekiel, and Daniel. As with any spiritual gift, the best prophet we can ever emulate is Jesus Christ. Take note of instances in Scripture where He prophesies. Write them down, and notice how people respond.

---

[66] "There we were, binding sheaves in the field. Then behold, my sheaf arose and also stood upright; and indeed your sheaves stood all around and bowed down to my sheaf." – Genesis 37:7

[67] Then he dreamed still another dream and told it to his brothers, and said, "Look, I have dreamed another dream. And this time, the sun, the moon, and the eleven stars bowed down to me." – Genesis 37:9

Jesus spoke words of encouragement in love to people who were eyebrow-deep in sin.

Second, get around prophetic people. We see the impact a prophetic community can have on bystanders in the life of Saul:

> *Then Saul sent messengers to take David. And when they saw the group of prophets prophesying, and Samuel standing as leader over them, the Spirit of God came upon the messengers of Saul, and they also prophesied. And when Saul was told, he sent other messengers, and they prophesied likewise. Then Saul sent messengers again the third time, and they prophesied also. Then he also went to Ramah...Then the Spirit of God was upon him also, and he went on and prophesied until he came to Naioth in Ramah. And he also stripped off his clothes and prophesied before Samuel in like manner...Therefore they say, "Is Saul also among the prophets?"* —1 Samuel 19:20-24

Saul wasn't a prophet; but when he got around prophetic people, he started prophesying! Find a church that believes in desiring and exercising spiritual gifts. Seek out a mentor who is familiar with the gift of prophecy, and invite him or her to comment on your spiritual disciplines. When you hear from God, let your mentor know what He's saying. Ask for advice on how to proceed: when, where, and with whom (if anyone) should you share the word?

Like any spiritual gift, the gift of prophecy will grow in your life as you practice it. If the Holy Spirit knows He can get a prophetic word *through* you, He will get more words *to* you! The greater demand you place on the anointing in your life, the more you will encounter the manifest presence of God's Holy Spirit. The more you ask to hear God's voice and make time to listen, the more He will speak!

Recommended Resources

Hagin, K. *Tongues: Beyond the Upper Room.* Tulsa: Faith
    Library Publications, 2007.
Wigglesworth, S. *Smith Wigglesworth on Spiritual Gifts.* New
    Kensington: Whitaker House, 1998.

CHAPTER 8

HEALING & MIRACLES

*But the manifestation of the Spirit is
given to each one for the profit of
all... to another gifts of healings by
the same Spirit, to another the
working of miracles...*

1 Corinthians 12:7, 9b-10a

Before I was introduced to the Spirit-filled life, reading the
first five books of the New Testament was more or less
like reading a history book. The miracles of Jesus and the
disciples recorded in the Gospels and the Book of Acts were
exciting to read about, yes, but they didn't really correspond to
anything in my experience. Like the Christians around me, I
believed these "signs and wonders" did actually occur two
thousand years ago. However, the general assumption of my
church community was that miracles were relegated to history. I
understood that Jesus had performed miracles in order to prove
He was the Son of God. Similarly, the apostles performed them
to prove Jesus had given them divine authority to build His
church. But I didn't really believe God performed miracles like
that anymore (unless it was in some far-off, undeveloped
country for a desperate missionary). He didn't need to! Now all
we needed was the Bible and modern medicine.

When I started attending a Spirit-filled church that believes
in miracles, it immediately became apparent to me that these
people had a completely different view of healing and miracles
than the one I had known growing up. Every week, the pastor
invited people who needed healing or a miracle to come up for
prayer. Church members shared testimony after testimony of

healings, miracles of provision, and other supernatural events that were happening in the here and now. I heard invitations to participate in different church outreaches where teams did "healing evangelism"—offering prayer for healing to people they met on the streets. In short, I discovered that healing and miracles can be—and *should be*—a *normal* and *central* part of Christian experience.

One day, while visiting a church in upstate New York, I stumbled across a book by John G. Lake, who was a healing evangelist in the early twentieth century.[68] After Lake's wife was miraculously healed in 1898 under the ministry of John Alexander Dowie, his life changed forever. He started to take God at His word, and believed that Jesus was willing to heal all who came to Him, all the time. He established Healing Rooms in Spokane, Washington, where anyone who needed physical healing could come and receive prayer.[69] Lake and his team of healing ministers published testimony after testimony of people who traveled from all over the country to receive prayer, and were miraculously and instantly healed. His ministry recorded over 100,000 healings in just five years. In fact, the Healing Rooms he started were so effective that the United States government dubbed Spokane the healthiest city in America.[70]

The book completely changed my paradigm for prayer. My soul cried out for more. Why couldn't the same miracles Lake saw *then* happen *now*? Why couldn't the same revival Lake experienced in Spokane, Washington, happen in New York City? All of a sudden, I was provoked to passionately pray for the things Jesus prayed for. I was done drifting through life wondering if God still heals. I wanted more at any cost!

---

[68] Lake, J. *John G. Lake on Healing*. New Kensington: Whitaker House, 2009.

[69] I would later learn that Lake inspired Cal & Michelle Pierce to start the International Association of Healing Rooms, also based in Spokane, Washington. To search for a Healing Rooms near you, go to healingrooms.com.

[70] https://healingrooms.com/index.php?page_id=422

Jesus' Ministry: Our Model

Lake's book, along with the vibrant Spirit-filled culture of my church, provoked me to search the Bible and listen closely to everything my pastor taught about healing and the miraculous. It wasn't long before I began to understand the framework of biblical truths that formed the basis for what I was experiencing.

The greatest "new" truth I learned was the idea that the purpose of Jesus' miraculous ministry was not just to demonstrate His divine nature as the Son of God. Jesus came not only as God to be worshiped and trusted for salvation; He came as our Elder Brother, the "Firstborn" and model for all reconciled sons and daughters of God. He not only put the Father's love on display; He also put our potential on display. This means that Christ's miraculous signs and wonders were not only confirmation of His divinity; they were also a template for the signs that should mark the life of every man and woman who puts their faith in Him and follows His example. Why else would He make statements like these?

> "And these signs will follow those who believe: In My name they will cast out demons; they will speak with new tongues; they will take up serpents; and if they drink anything deadly, it will by no means hurt them; they will lay hands on the sick, and they will recover." —Mark 16:17-18

> "Most assuredly, I say to you, he who believes in Me, the works that I do he will do also; and greater works than these he will do, because I go to My Father." — John 14:12

We find several proofs in the New Testament that Jesus' miracle ministry was the model and mandate for all believers. First, (as we saw in Chapter 2) the Gospels and Acts show us that the Holy Spirit who rested upon Jesus is the same Spirit who baptizes us. After all, there is only one Holy Spirit! We have already taken note of the fact that Jesus' miracle ministry did not begin until after the Holy Spirit descended upon Him at His baptism, for a reason. It was at this point that Jesus became anointed by God with the Holy Spirit to do miracles: "...God anointed Jesus of Nazareth with the Holy Spirit and with power, who went about doing good and healing all who were oppressed by the devil, for God was with Him" (Acts 10:38).

Then, before His ascension, Jesus told His disciples to wait in Jerusalem for the *same* Holy Spirit to come upon them with power:

> *"But you shall receive power when the Holy Spirit has come upon you; and you shall be witnesses to Me in Jerusalem, and in all Judea and Samaria, and to the end of the earth."* — Acts 1:8

Jesus makes it clear that there is a fundamental connection between receiving the power of God through the baptism in the Holy Spirit and becoming His witnesses. A witness of Christ is one who can give testimony that He is who He says He is—with convincing proof. In a court of law, a witness who offers a testimony without proof will not be taken seriously. How can Christians witness to the reality of salvation and their Spirit-filled life without demonstrating the power of the Holy Spirit?

In his epistles, the apostle Paul was clear that in his ministry, the preaching of the gospel was always accompanied by demonstrations of the Spirit and power (miracles):

> *For I decided to know nothing among you except Jesus Christ and him crucified. And I was with you in weakness and in fear and much trembling, and my speech and my message were not in plausible words of wisdom, but in demonstration of the Spirit and of power, so that your faith might not rest in the wisdom of men but in the power of God.* — 1 Corinthians 2:2-5

For I will not venture to speak of anything except what Christ has accomplished through me to bring the Gentiles to obedience—by word and deed, by the power of signs and wonders, by the power of the Spirit of God—so that from Jerusalem and all the way around to Illyricum I have fulfilled the ministry of the gospel of Christ... —Romans 15:18-19

For our gospel did not come to you in word only, but also in power, and in the Holy Spirit and in much assurance, as you know what kind of men we were among you for your sake. —1 Thessalonians 1:5

If Paul said, "Imitate me, just as I also imitate Christ" (1 Corinthians 11:1), then we are called to follow Jesus' example of preaching the gospel with the Spirit and power.

The second proof that we are expected to imitate Jesus' miraculous ministry is seen in the progression by which Jesus authorized increasing numbers of His disciples to represent Him as partners in His ministry—a progression that ultimately includes us. Let's follow the sequence in the Gospel accounts.

For starters, we must acknowledge that Jesus Christ has all authority:

And Jesus came and spoke to them, saying, "All authority has been given to Me in heaven and on earth..." —Matthew 28:18

Because Jesus had authority, He could give authority. He first extended it to His twelve disciples:

Then He called His twelve disciples together and gave them power and authority over all demons, and to cure diseases. He sent them to preach the kingdom of God and to heal the sick. —Luke 9:1-2

Shortly after this, Jesus expanded this number to include another seventy:

After these things the Lord appointed seventy others also, and sent them two by two before His face into every city and place where He Himself was about to go. —Luke 10:1

Jesus anointed these seventy disciples to go before Him, heal the sick, and preach the gospel. He called them into a life of preparing the unsaved for Jesus' imminent arrival.

Finally, immediately before his ascension into heaven, Jesus distributed His power and authority to *all believers*:

And He said to them, "Go into all the world and preach the gospel to every creature. He who believes and is baptized will be saved; but he who does not believe will be condemned. And these signs will follow those who believe: In My name they will cast out demons; they will speak with new tongues; they will take up serpents; and if they drink anything deadly, it will by no means hurt them; they will lay hands on the sick, and they will recover." —Mark 16:15-18

We also see how Christ's authority is meant to extend to us in the Great Commission of Matthew 28:18-20:

And Jesus came and spoke to them, saying, "All authority has been given to Me in heaven and on earth. Go therefore and make disciples of all the nations, baptizing them in the name of the Father and of the Son and of the Holy Spirit, teaching them to observe all things that I have commanded you; and lo, I am with you always, even to the end of the age."

As disciples of Christ, we are to "observe all things" commanded by Christ. Undoubtedly this includes the command to believe in Christ, and the expectation to see accompanying signs and wonders as evidence of our faith.

The third proof that healing and miracles are to flow through our lives as Spirit-filled, Spirit-empowered witnesses of Christ is simply that miracles express and demonstrate the gospel. The miracles Christ performed were not merely displays of power, or magic tricks to convince His audience that He had supernatural abilities. The Bible says His miracles were *signs*. Signs of what? They were signs of the mission He had been sent to accomplish here on earth.

The Son of God came to save sinners from death and hell and restore us to eternal life and relationship with the Father. Therefore He performed acts that expressed 1) compassion for those who were perishing, 2) dominion over the devil, and 3) restoration of bodies, souls, and spirits to wholeness and eternal life. Sickness, disease, demonic oppression, and death came into the world through sin. By healing the sick and diseased, casting out demons, and raising the dead, Jesus revealed the true effects of the salvation He would go to the cross to accomplish.

Along with pointing to the atoning, restorative work of the cross, Jesus' miracles also pointed to the coming kingdom of God. Consider the miracles of provision Jesus performed. He provided top-shelf wine at a wedding, bread and fish on at least two occasions for crowds of thousands, and money for His and His disciples' taxes (pulled from a fish's mouth!), among others. In each of these miracles, the kingdom—the realm that expresses God's generous abundance and utter freedom from all fear of lack—became real on earth. Or consider Jesus' miraculous calming of the storm in Mark 4. When He spoke the words "Peace, be still!" (Mark 4:39) over the raging seas, He brought the created order under the rule and reign of God's kingdom of peace.

As witnesses to the gospel and ambassadors of the kingdom, and as the living, breathing body of Christ on the earth, we are called to continue Christ's work of bringing healing, freedom, restoration, wholeness, peace, and abundance to people's lives.

You See What You Expect To See

Before I believed that the Holy Spirit's gifts of healing and miracles were still active today, I didn't really see or hear of healings or miracles taking place. However, once I stepped into an environment of faith for healing and miracles, my eyes were opened. Since that time, I have seen dozens of miracles myself, and heard testimonies of thousands more.

Several years ago, my wife and I started the Healing Rooms ministry at our church. Every month, we get together with a group of phenomenally anointed volunteers and pray for the sick. We have seen people walk into the Healing Rooms leaning on canes, and walk out without having to use them. We have seen curved spines cured of scoliosis. We have seen bone spurs shrink away, and stunted limbs sprout out of healed bodies. We've seen Jesus dissolve terminal cancers on multiple occasions. We even saw a precious one-month-old girl healed of a life-threatening liver disease!

I'll never forget the day Amanda walked into the Healing Rooms. Her mom had given birth prematurely at 26 weeks, and a severe head bleed had affected the entire left side of Amanda's body. Her left lung had collapsed, and her left leg was almost six inches shorter than her right leg because her femur had grown incorrectly.

But God changed all that. As we prayed for Amanda, we watched her left leg grow. By the time we were done praying, her left leg was exactly the same length as her right leg. Jesus healed her leg completely! We encouraged her to go to her doctor and confirm everything God had done in her body. When she went to visit her doctor that Monday, she didn't tell him anything about getting prayer. She simply let him measure the distance between each of her hips and the floor, just as he had done before. He was shocked! Amanda became an amazing testimony of the way Jesus is willing to heal when we give Him the chance.

If you have yet to see or experience a miracle of God, then I would ask you, what is your level of expectation? In particular, what do your prayers sound like when you encounter a problem or impossibility? Jesus told us to expect miraculous things when we pray:

> *"For assuredly, I say to you, whoever says to this mountain, 'Be removed and be cast into the sea,' and does not doubt in his heart, but believes that those things he says will be done, he will have whatever he says. Therefore I say to you, whatever things you ask when you pray, believe that you receive them, and you will have them.'" —Mark 11:23-24*

God asks us to believe that we can really move mountains. There is no point in praying for signs, miracles, and wonders if we don't actually believe our prayers have power.

Jesus' requirements for our faith should *make us uncomfortable*. Most of us have to admit that we *do* have doubts in our heart when it comes to believing God as fully as we should. The good news is that while God does call us to extreme faith, He can start working with whatever measure of faith we offer Him. Did you know Jesus gives us permission to ask for more faith? In Mark 9, the father of a demonized child asks Jesus if He can do anything about his son's condition. Jesus says to him, "If you can believe, all things are possible to him who believes" (Mark 9:23). In response, the man cries, "Lord, I believe; help my unbelief!" (Mark 9:24). This is a prayer we should never be embarrassed to pray! God will cure our unbelief, just as He will cure our bodies.

One of the ways we should feed and challenge our faith is by consistently studying the miracle accounts in the New Testament and inviting the Holy Spirit to give us faith to expect

Him to do the same things through us. Take this account of a young man named Eutychus, for example:

> *Now on the first day of the week, when the disciples came together to break bread, Paul, ready to depart the next day, spoke to them and continued his message until midnight. There were many lamps in the upper room where they were gathered together. And in a window sat a certain young man named Eutychus, who was sinking into a deep sleep. He was overcome by sleep; and as Paul continued speaking, he fell down from the third story and was taken up dead. But Paul went down, fell on him, and embracing him said, "Do not trouble yourselves, for his life is in him." Now when he had come up, had broken bread and eaten, and talked a long while, even till daybreak, he departed. And they brought the young man in alive, and they were not a little comforted.* —Acts 20:7-12

Eutychus picked the worst seat for a long sermon—he was literally bored to death. He drifted off into sleep and fell three stories onto the ground below. Dead. If you had been in this meeting, what do you think your level of faith would have led you to do? Call an ambulance? Gather around him, feel bad, console his family, and make vague but well-intentioned remarks that you were sure Eutychus was in a "better place?"

Look at Paul's response. He falls on the boy, embraces him, and declares with full confidence that Eutychus is still alive. Sure enough, there he was, alive and sitting in the meeting the next morning. Paul knew the Spirit of resurrection lived in him and worked through him. And so should we!

There are eighteen miracles described in the Book of Acts. Remember: Acts takes place *after* Jesus had already ascended into heaven. The Holy Spirit caused all the miracles in Acts to take place, but the disciples were the ones who saw them happening through their own hands! Paul's handkerchiefs and aprons were so anointed that whenever someone touched them, "...diseases left them and the evil spirits went out of them"

(Acts 19:12). Peter's *shadow* was so anointed "...that they brought the sick out into the streets and laid them on beds and couches, that at least the shadow of Peter passing by might fall on some of them" (Acts 5:15).

What made the early church so special? They *believed* God would confirm His word with signs and wonders. They took Jesus at His word:

> So then, after the Lord had spoken to them, He was received up into heaven, and sat down at the right hand of God. And [His disciples] went out and preached everywhere, the Lord working with them and confirming the word through the accompanying signs. Amen. —Mark 16:19-20

The only reason the modern church is so different from the early church is that we've lost that belief. We preach the gospel without any expectation that God will confirm His word with signs and wonders after we're done speaking. Instead of standing on His Word and waiting for supernatural things to take place, we quickly take our seats after the sermon. So many of us have slid into nominal Christianity—a life devoid of God's resurrection power—because we have lost our expectation for God's Holy Spirit to move in our lives. It's time for us to rediscover true faith.

Our current generation is, by default, the beneficiary of more testimonies of God's amazing power than any generation before us. We not only read about God's great power in our Bibles and history books—all we have to do is turn on the TV or scroll through our Instagram feed to see the amazing miracles God's Holy Spirit is still working today through the hands of His disciples. So if you're sitting on the sidelines, waiting for God to do something miraculous to you, let me ask you this: isn't your butt getting a little sore? Aren't your excuses getting a little tired and played out? You have the same Holy Spirit who raised Jesus

Christ from the dead in YOU! Get up and ask the Holy Spirit to show you someone He wants you to pray for!

What Happens When It Doesn't Happen?

It's vital to be led by the Spirit as you move in His gifts of healing and miracles. One of the things we see in the individual miracle accounts in the Gospels is that Jesus never healed two people exactly the same way! He always followed the Holy Spirit and received His leading for how to minister to each person as a unique individual, and we should do the same. God does not operate by formula; He moves by faith.

Jesus never asked the Father if it was His will to heal someone. That much was settled—as it should be for us. We don't have to *guess* at God's will regarding healing. We are exhorted to *know* God's will through study of His Word and direct communication with His Holy Spirit.

Mark tells the story of a leprous man who approached Jesus Christ and asked for healing:

> *Now a leper came to Him, imploring Him, kneeling down to Him and saying to Him, "If You are willing, You can make me clean." —Mark 1:40*

This was a completely acceptable statement for the leper to make because Jesus had not yet demonstrated His will. Jesus responded immediately, and in doing so, He responded in a way that set a precedent for the way we are meant to pray as His followers:

> *Then Jesus, moved with compassion, stretched out His hand and touched him, and said to him, "I am willing; be cleansed." As soon as He had spoken, immediately the leprosy left him, and he was cleansed. —Mark 1:41-42*

Jesus' response forever answers the question, "Is it God's will to heal?" It is still—and always will be—God's will to heal His children. If salvation is still for today, healing is still for today! Provision was made for both on the cross. Whenever we see a written record of Jesus doing something in His ministry, we should pray for and pursue that thing with the same confidence we have when we pray for salvation. Our prayers should not start with, "If You are willing," but rather, "Because I know it is Your will." God has left us ample demonstration of His will, along with instructions to earnestly contend for the things He has promised us.

When we step out in faith and obedience to minister to someone, it's appropriate to expect to see results. In fact, it would be crazy not to! However, there will be times when we don't immediately see the results we expect. Sometimes when we pray for someone who's sick, he still goes home sick. Sometimes when we pray for someone struggling financially, she still comes up short on rent. In these cases, all we must do is ask the Holy Spirit if there's anything else He wants us to do. Sometimes He simply wants us to wait, because the results are coming. Sometimes He wants us to pray again. And sometimes He wants us to simply live in the mystery of knowing that our responsibility is to be obedient and faithful to do what He asks, and His job is to bring the results, whether we see them or not. No matter what we see before our eyes, we are to train our faith, obedience, and expectation to align consistently with His character, His promises, and His call on our lives.

Miracles in the Church

One of the sobering things we see in the Gospels is that not everyone was excited about the healings and miracles Jesus performed. While it was obvious to most of Jesus' audience that "no one [could] do these signs that [He did] unless God [was] with him" (John 3:2), the Jewish religious leaders repeatedly challenged Jesus as to where He received His authority and power to perform miracles. On one dramatic occasion, the religious leaders actually accused Jesus of getting His power from the devil.[71] Significantly, this was the occasion on which Jesus made His warning about the sin of blaspheming the Holy Spirit. It is blasphemy to attribute the work of the Holy Spirit to the devil. When we disbelieve, resist, or try to shut down the supernatural work of the Holy Spirit, we are actually aligning with an *antichrist* spirit. The name Christ comes from the Greek word for "Anointed One." Jesus was called the Christ precisely because He was anointed by the Holy Spirit. Any opposition to that anointing—the same anointing that rests on Spirit-filled believers—is antichrist in nature.

The enemy has a definitive agenda of shutting down all the gifts of the Holy Spirit, and he works overtime to promote unbelief in the church. And consistent with Jesus' experience, some of the people Satan uses to carry out this agenda are actually leaders in the church! In many cases, these leaders have no intention of opposing God—they seek to defend what they believe to be true. However, for a variety of reasons (bad teaching, their own fears and unbelief, etc.) they end up in a position where they are standing against a person who is moving in the power of the Spirit.

In one of his sermons,[72] John G. Lake tells the story of Andrew Murray, the Lead Pastor of the Dutch Reformed Church of South Africa. Doctors pronounced Murray incurable of "preacher's throat." This was a terrible condition for a pastor to have, as it would eventually leave him without the ability to speak, and of course unable to address his congregation. Even

---

[71] "Now when the Pharisees heard it they said, 'This fellow does not cast out demons except by Beelzebub, the ruler of the demons.'" – Matthew 12:24

[72] "Divine Healing" preached at the Dutch Church Hall in Somerset East, South Africa, in October, 1910.

after traveling to London to see specialists for his condition, he was left without hope.

Out of ideas and running out of hope, he visited the Bethshan Divine Healing Mission while on a trip to London to receive prayer. That day, his life completely changed. He was completely healed! He wrote a book called *Divine Healing*,[73] which was extensively circulated in South Africa, and the whole denomination was transformed as a result of his experience. People all over the country started asking their local pastors to pray for healing.

Tragically, the local pastors *didn't have faith for healing*. They hadn't had the same experience as Andrew Murray, and they didn't feel adequately empowered to contend for healing. Those who didn't see healing happen immediately were ashamed and embarrassed. Instead of humbly asking God for an increased anointing to pray for healing, the local pastors demanded that Murray's book be taken out of circulation. Murray was requested not to teach divine healing in the Dutch Reformed Church of South Africa from that time forward. The congregants of an entire denomination were robbed of their expectation for— and experience of—the miraculous, because of unwillingness on the part of local pastors to contend for supernatural manifestations to take place.

In the Western church, particularly in the United States, many Christians have come under the influence of the false doctrine of cessationism. This doctrine claims that the gifts of the Spirit and the miracles performed by Jesus and the apostles ceased when the last of the original apostles died. The problem with cessationism is that the Bible *never says* that the miraculous ministry of the Spirit will cease before the Second Coming of Jesus Christ. The only time Paul uses the word "cease" is in 1 Corinthians 13:

---

[71] This book is now published under a different name: Murray, A. *Healing Secrets*. New Kensington: Whitaker House, 2004.

Love never fails. But whether there are prophecies, they will fail; whether there are tongues, they will cease; whether there is knowledge, it will vanish away. For we know in part and we prophesy in part. But when that which is perfect has come, then that which is in part will be done away... For now we see in a mirror, dimly, but then face to face. Now I know in part, but then I shall know just as I also am known. —
1 Corinthians 13:8-10, 12

Paul is clearly speaking of the day when we will see God "face to face"—either in heaven, or when Jesus comes again. When we are perfected and experience heavenly reality in its fullness, the role of gifts of the Spirit in our lives will be completed. Until, then, we still need them!

Cessationism is a manmade theory added on to the Scriptures in order to explain why we don't see the same miracles we read about in the Bible. When Paul outlines the five-fold ministry to the church at Ephesus, he doesn't say that only twelve men were created to be apostles; he says that God gave, "...some to be apostles, some prophets, some evangelists, and some pastors and teachers" (Ephesians 4:11). When God poured out His Holy Spirit, He did poured it out on "all flesh" (Joel 2:28); not just twelve men. The same Holy Spirit who filled the original twelve apostles to walk in supernatural power and authority lives in each and every single Christian!

Revival & Renewal

Throughout history, the Holy Spirit has continually been at work to renew the church and call her back to true faith and power. Since the days of the early church, seasons of spiritual revival have always been breaking out somewhere. Every revival has similar features—increased spiritual hunger, conviction of and repentance for sin, increased devotion and passion for God, new believers coming to faith, and many kinds of signs and wonders.

Arguably, the greatest global revival in the last fifty years traces back to the outpouring of the Spirit that began in Toronto, Canada. Along with a renewal of all the gifts of the Spirit we have studied so far, some of the common manifestations seen in this revival include laughter and "drunkenness" in the Holy Spirit.

Significantly, the first accusation brought against the early church after its members were filled with the Holy Spirit was one of drunken behavior. The multitude began speaking in tongues and outsiders mocked them, saying, "They are full of new wine" (Acts 2:13). Peter had to stand up and defend them, explaining that they were not drunk, but rather demonstrating the fullness of the Holy Spirit as promised by the prophet Joel.[74] I believe that accusation was very intentionally included in the narrative of the Holy Spirit's activity in the early church as recorded by Luke. When I picture this scene, I imagine the early church not only speaking in tongues, but also completely overwhelmed by the presence of God Himself: laughing, dancing, singing, shouting, and even falling all over themselves trying to come to terms with this new spiritual reality.

The Bible compares the symptoms of the Holy Spirit working in us during times of worship to "drunkenness" on several occasions. In Ephesians 5:18, Paul instructs the church at Ephesus with the following: "...do not be drunk with wine, in which is dissipation; but be filled with the Spirit..." This comparison to consuming alcohol in excess is done intentionally. When we drink, our body releases neurotransmitters such as serotonin and dopamine that serve to increase pleasure in our

---

[74] "And it shall come to pass afterward that I will pour out My Spirit on all flesh; your sons and your daughters shall prophesy, your old men shall dream dreams, your young men shall see visions. And also on My menservants and on My maidservants I will pour out My Spirit in those days. And I will show wonders in the heavens and in the earth..." – Joel 2:28-30a

bodies. The result is reduced inhibition, joy that defies circumstance (also known as positive affect), and…you guessed it…laughing! What's my point? The presence of God should make us feel *good*! Encountering Him should fill us with overflowing joy.

Are all the manifestations in a Charismatic renewal service evidence of encountering the presence of God? No. Sometimes people are just being emotional, and sometimes they are actually manifesting another spirit. So how should we respond to these situations?

No church is perfectly zealous. So, odds are you will have to make a choice: would you rather be in a body of over-zealous or under-zealous believers? Personally, I would take over-zealous any day. Isn't it worth it to put up with the occasional over-zealous manifestation if it inspires people to passionately pursue God and expect Him to touch them in a cognition-shattering way?

We also have to realize the shortcomings of our own powers of observation. Can we really claim to know what is best—the *ideal* setting for an encounter with God—for everyone in the room? On some occasions, it's impossible see what God is doing with someone who is manifesting. Sometimes a person who is having a demonic manifestation is getting delivered of demonic oppression. Sometimes the person who is laughing out of control in a church service is actually being healed of years of depression and abuse. And sometimes the "charismania"—whether laughter, dancing, or any other brand of enthusiasm—that we assume will offend people actually affects them in the opposite way and draws them into a personal relationship with Jesus Christ.

In revival, the Holy Spirit is intent on confronting the "boxes" we try to put Him in. He is more than willing to offend our mind to expose our heart. When we are exposed to manifestations of the Spirit that we don't understand or that offend what we thought we knew about God, we have a choice. Will we cling to our old paradigm, or will we allow the Holy Spirit to lead us into His new reality? If having a church where the Holy Spirit is active means allowing Him to move however He wants, will we say, "Lord, more of You at any cost?"

Recommended Resources

Bosworth, F.F. *Christ the Healer.* Ada: Chosen Books, 2008.

Lake, J. *John G. Lake on Healing.* New Kensington: Whitaker House, 2009.

CHAPTER 9

LIFE IN A SPIRIT-FILLED COMMUNITY

For as we have many members in one body,
but all the members do not have the same function,
so we, being many, are one body in Christ,
and individually members of one another.

Romans 12:4-5

Paul explained how the gifts of the Holy Spirit are designed to function with a metaphor everyone can understand—the human body:

> *For as the body is one and has many members, but all the members of that one body, being many, are one body, so also is Christ. For by one Spirit we were all baptized into one body—whether Jews or Greeks, whether slaves or free—and have all been made to drink into one Spirit... —1 Corinthians 12:12-13*

The beauty of this metaphor is that it paints a perfect picture of integrity, unity, and diversity. Every part of our body is unique and vital—as long as it is functioning where it belongs in the body, in harmony with the other parts. Separated from the body, each part loses both its life and its purpose. In the same way, each individual Christian has incredible gifts, value, and purpose, but those things can only be expressed and fulfilled in the context of life-giving connection in the whole body of Christ.

The Spirit-filled *life* is designed to function in the context of Spirit-filled *community*. Paul says we "were all baptized into one body...and have all been made to drink into one Spirit." When you were baptized—both in water and in the Holy Spirit—you weren't just baptized into a new *individual* life, identity, calling, purpose, and ministry. You were baptized into a body—the entire global community of believers! You don't just belong to Christ; you belong to His family, the Church; and this membership comes with certain responsibilities and benefits that are vital to understand.

The Church

The first thing to understand about what it means to belong to the body of Christ is this: *you need to be in fellowship with other believers.*

There are too many lone ranger Christians out there these days, telling themselves that reading books, playing worship albums, and listening to sermons online are all they need to grow in their faith. Many of these people had a bad experience at church and decided they were done with church altogether. While bad church experiences are unfortunately common (every one of us, in fact, will be hurt by another Christian at some point, because we're human), abandoning fellowship with other believers makes you even more vulnerable to spiritual shipwreck. None of us gets to live in our own little bubble with Jesus. Why? Because *Jesus Himself designed us to grow in fellowship with the members of His body.*

Paul describes this design in his letter to the Ephesians:

> *And He Himself gave some to be apostles, some prophets, some evangelists, and some pastors and teachers, for the equipping of the saints for the work of ministry, for the edifying of the body of Christ, till we all come to the unity of the faith and of the knowledge of the Son of God, to a perfect man, to the measure of the stature of the fullness of Christ; that we should no longer be children, tossed to and fro and carried about with every wind of doctrine, by the trickery of men, in the cunning craftiness of deceitful plotting, but, speaking the truth in love, may grow up in all things*

> *into Him who is the head—Christ—from whom the*
> *whole body, joined and knit together by what every*
> *joint supplies, according to the effective working by*
> *which every part does its share, causes growth of the*
> *body for the edifying of itself in love. —Ephesians*
> *4:11-16*

Wow. Look at those verses—that is all *one sentence*. This is one big thought about how Jesus designed His body to function and grow into its destiny and potential. We see that Jesus has appointed people to certain leadership roles—the "five-fold" ministry of apostles, prophets, teachers, pastors, and evangelists—to equip and edify the saints. This ministry takes us out of immaturity, where we are vulnerable to deception, and into maturity, which looks like:

- Unity of faith
- Knowledge of Jesus
- Speaking the truth in love
- Loving one another like Jesus and looking like Him in every way

Only when we are "joined and knit together" can this growth process work in our lives and bring us to maturity. That means being in relationship. "Fellowship" means so much more than just sitting in the same room as other Christians on Sunday morning. It means having brothers and sisters in Christ who know you, share life with you, and encourage you in your faith—as you do the same for them.

Yes, relationships can be messy. That's true both in church and in your daily life. The body of Christ is not a place where there are no relational messes—but it is a place where we have unique resources and tools to clean up these messes and learn how we can prevent more of them in the future.

Leadership in the Body

The next thing to understand about belonging to the body of Christ is how God designed leadership to function in His body. The passage above from Ephesians tells us that God has appointed individuals with certain gifts "for the equipping of the saints for the work of ministry." The primary role of the leaders in the body is to teach and train the congregation (laypeople) to minister to God, to one another, and to the world.

Unfortunately, many churches treat their leaders, not the "saints," as the ones who are primarily called to do the work of ministry. Historically in these churches, the priest (or another figurehead) has been understood to be the intermediary between God and man. In these cases, the priest is the only one who can perform certain rituals, administer absolution of sin, and teach the Word of God. This type of leadership creates two unhealthy dynamics in the church. First, it requires the members of the congregation to depend on the priest for education, spiritual direction, and ultimate meaning. Second, it encourages the belief that the priests are just a little more "holy" than the laypeople (congregation).

The New Testament clearly teaches that every believer in Jesus is a member of "a royal priesthood" (1 Peter 2:9) and that there is only "one Mediator between God and men, the Man Christ Jesus" (1 Timothy 2:5). We are *all* called to be priests who can minister directly to God and the world through Christ. We can come directly before the "throne of grace" to receive mercy and forgiveness for sin (Hebrews 4:16). And we all have the indwelling, empowering Holy Spirit, who enables us to hear from and communicate with God directly and minister with His gifts—gifts that we can use both inside and outside the church building. In fact, we are called to do the "work of ministry" in every area of our lives. For Spirit-filled believers, there is to be no divide between sacred and secular areas of life. We are to see the Spirit-filled janitor as being just as holy and as much a minister as a local pastor or popular Christian speaker. There are no first and second-class roles in God's kingdom.

As a pastor, I understand that my job is to *put myself out of a job.* My responsibility is to raise up men and women of God who can preach the gospel and pastor other people just as effectively as I can. I want to teach the people at CityLight Church that if I can do it, they can do it. And what I really *don't* want to do is teach them to depend on me instead of Jesus Christ, or to think that my walk as a follower of Christ is unattainable for them.

Pastors or priests who foster a culture of dependency in their churches create a bottleneck that limits their own effectiveness and that of their churches. This is what we see happening in Exodus 18. Moses' father-in-law, Jethro, observes how Moses is leading the people of Israel, and immediately recognizes that his leadership approach is unsustainable. Because Moses was the one who knew the standard God set for Israel, he was singlehandedly trying to address all the legal matters for God's people. Jethro pointed out that Moses would burn himself out by taking on the burdens of all the people, and the people, too, would also become burned out by conceding decision-making authority to Moses.

Moses listened to Jethro and fixed the problem by changing his approach in two ways. First, he taught *all* the people God's law so they could make most everyday decisions themselves. Then, he appointed anointed leaders over lower-level courts to interpret smaller matters. Moses was left to bear the decision-making burden only in extremely difficult cases where it was otherwise impossible to determine God's will.

From the moment Moses began to teach God's word to the people of Israel, they became properly equipped to establish their own personal relationships with God. The result was not only the capacity to make sound decisions for themselves, but also the ability to build faith through a genuine relationship with their loving Father.

Church leaders are called take the same approach. Their goal should be to give people the knowledge, tools, and training necessary to connect to God, walk faithfully with Him, make great decisions, and minister to others. This is how they equip the body to be healthy and grow strong and mature.

Covenant

A third thing we need to understand about being a member of the body of Christ is that this is a *covenant* relationship.

As we saw earlier, the New Testament uses the term "adoption" to describe the New Covenant relationship God has established with us through Jesus Christ. Adoption is a covenant relationship. When a child is adopted, his relationship with his new parents is personal, legal, and permanent. Because of this, if those parents have any other children, the adopted child becomes a full sibling to those children. The same is true with us as God's adopted children. Our covenant relationship with God through Jesus not only binds us to Him for life; it also makes us permanent brothers and sisters with one another.

This point is important because it adds another dimension to understanding how we are to approach our relationships with other believers. As members of the same *body*, we recognize that we need one another in order to grow and become healthy and mature in God. As members of the same *family*, we recognize that we owe one another honor and loyalty as we interact, especially when we have disagreements or conflict. Instead of cutting off relationships, we are called to repent, forgive, repair, and reconcile with our brothers and sisters in Christ.

In Western society, the concept of a covenant is all but lost. Marriage used to be that kind of personal, legal, and permanent relationship, but since the Sexual Revolution it has morphed from "as long as we both shall live" to "as long as we both shall love." Our level of hope and expectation for relationships to last is at an extreme low point, and this attitude has certainly spilled over into the church. Many people approach church with an individualistic, consumer mentality that says, "I'm really just here for me. If I'm not getting 'fed,' or if I have a bad experience with someone here, I'm moving on."

The sad thing about carrying this attitude is that it ultimately leaves people brokenhearted and alone. We were created for relationships—relationships that are deeply connected, loving, supportive, and enduring. We were created for covenant. If we're honest with ourselves, we all deeply long to be part of a healthy family. This may seem impossible based on our experience, but the Holy Spirit is intent on restoring that hope—and its fulfillment—in the hearts of the Father's sons and daughters. This is, in fact, the Holy Spirit's mission on the earth—to restore the family of God.

The Standard of Love

God has given us a defining standard for how we are to treat one another as members of His body and family. In the Old Testament, the standard was, "...you shall love your neighbor as yourself..." (Leviticus 19:18). But in the New Testament, Jesus said, "A new commandment I give to you, that you love one another; as I have loved you, that you also love one another" (John 13:34). We are not just to love others as we love ourselves; we are to love them as *Jesus loves us.*

Like every command of God, the command to love like Jesus is impossible to follow alone, but feasible as we lean on Him. If we trust Jesus and depend on His Spirit to lead and empower us, we will grow up, like Paul said in Ephesians, to "the stature of the fullness of Christ" (Ephesians 4:13). No matter how many growing pains we have to endure along the way, if we keep pursuing the depths of God's love, we will learn to love like Jesus.

One important thing to remember is that we can only give away what we have first received. In order to love like Jesus, we must receive His love for ourselves. As 1 John 4:19 says, "We love Him because He first loved us." If we want to love like He loves, then we need to pursue ongoing revelation of, and enduring encounters with, His infinite love.

How He Loves

Jesus loves us in more ways than we can count, but here are five important ways we can imitate His love in our relationships with each other:

Jesus separates us from our sin. The phrase "love the sinner; hate the sin" has come under criticism, but it is absolutely biblical. On the one hand, if we say we love the sinner *and* the sin, then it's not really love; for you can't love something that distorts and destroys the one you love. On the other hand, if you hate the sin *and* the sinner, then you clearly don't align with the God who "so loved the world" (John 3:16). And if you love the sin and hate the sinner, well, then you're really in trouble.

The only reason people struggle with "love the sinner; hate the sin" is because they haven't yet come to terms with sin. They don't yet see how the cancer of sin is destroying their lives. But Jesus sees it clearly. His love is never distorted so that it becomes too hard on the sinner or too soft on sin. When we rely on the Holy Spirit, we too can learn to see one another through His lens of love.

Jesus forgave our sin. He forgave all of it—past, present, and future—and He expects us to do the same for others. Throughout the Gospels, Jesus repeatedly makes the standard for forgiveness abundantly clear. We are to forgive everyone, every time. If we do not, we will not be forgiven:

For if you forgive men their trespasses, your heavenly Father will also forgive you. But if you do not forgive men their trespasses, neither will your Father forgive your trespasses. —Matthew 6:14-15

Jesus has the same "no tolerance" policy with unforgiveness in our lives that He does with sin, and for good reason. Holding bitter judgments and resentment in our hearts towards our brothers and sisters opens the door of our hearts wide to the enemy. Forgiveness is for *our* sake as much as the person we forgive. Forgiving sets our hearts free and enables us to continually repair our relationships with one another.

Jesus trusts us. In fact, Jesus trusts us more than we trust ourselves. If you need proof of this, consider this. Jesus took a group of young, blue-collar guys—His disciples—and spent three power-packed years training them for the future. Though He warned them that He had come to die, they had no clue that He would be leaving them after such a short time. Then, after the world-shattering experience of the crucifixion and resurrection, Jesus dropped another bomb on them. He was heading back to heaven and handing the baton off to them! Jesus trusted this small group of disciples with His entire global ministry. How many leaders would come up with a succession plan like this?

Why did Jesus trust them, and why does He trust us? First, Jesus trusts us because His trust is not based on us; it is based on Him. Like His love, God's trust is unconditional. It's a choice He makes because He wants to make it. Second, Jesus trusts us because *He trusts Himself in us.* When Jesus ascended to the Father, He didn't leave us alone—He sent His own Spirit to live in us. That Spirit is bringing about the purposes of God in us—not in spite of our weakness, lack, or problems, but in and through them. For two thousand years, He has been building His church through the same kind of people He started with, and shows no sign of changing His approach.

Jesus desires that we would trust our brothers and sisters in the same way—not on the basis of their actions, but because we freely choose to open our hearts and lives to them, and because we trust God in them. Trusting God in people helps us to see and invite the best in others to come to the surface. The body of Christ should be a place where people feel *believed in*.

Jesus serves us. At the Last Supper, Jesus began the evening by serving His disciples in a way that shocked them:

> *Jesus, knowing that the Father had given all things into His hands, and that He had come from God and was going to God, rose from supper and laid aside His garments, took a towel and girded Himself. After that, He poured water into a basin and began to wash the disciples' feet, and to wipe them with the towel with which He was girded…*
>
> *So when He had washed their feet, taken His garments, and sat down again, He said to them, "Do you know what I have done to you? You call Me Teacher and Lord, and you say well, for so I am. If I then, your Lord and Teacher, have washed your feet, you also ought to wash one another's feet. For I have given you an example, that you should do as I have done to you." —John 13:3-5, 12-15*

Foot washing was a task for the lowliest of servants. Yet Jesus humbled Himself to perform a task the disciples wouldn't have even performed for each other. Then He explained what it meant: "This is how I want you to serve one another."

On several prior occasions, Jesus explained to His disciples that serving is what defines "greatness" in the kingdom of God:

> *"You know that the rulers of the Gentiles lord it over them, and those who are great exercise authority over them. Yet it shall not be so among you; but whoever desires to become great among you, let him be your servant. And whoever desires to be first among you, let him be your slave—just as the Son of Man did not come to be served, but to serve, and to give His life a ransom for many." —Matthew 20:22-25*

It seems paradoxical that taking the "low road" would be the path of greatness, but that is because we aren't used to thinking like God thinks. Worldly kings seek greatness through dominance, but the King of Kings demonstrates greatness through radical service—and He wants His sons and daughters to follow His example.

Jesus lays down His life for us. Laying your life down elevates service to the realm of sacrifice. Jesus Himself said, "Greater love has no one than this, than to lay down one's life for his friends" (John 15:13). Though none of us can be called to die the infinite death Jesus died for our sins, there are other ways we can put everything on the line for one another. Laying our lives down looks like being there for one another when it's not convenient. It looks like weeping with those who weep, and rejoicing with those who rejoice. It looks like giving extravagantly of our time, talent, and treasure to help those around us. It looks like making friends with the poor, rejected, and lonely. It looks like Jesus.

Levels and Kinds of Relationship

Loving others like Jesus will look different according to the level and kind of relationship you have with a person. Though we are members of a global body of Christ and called to love everyone, that doesn't mean we are going to be best friends with everyone in church.

When we look at Jesus' life and ministry in Scripture, we see that even He had different levels and kinds of relationship in His life. He preached and ministered to crowds. He had a larger group of disciples, and within that group, the twelve with whom He traveled and partnered most closely. Among the twelve, Peter, James, and John—the "Dream Team"—seemed to have a special level of friendship with Jesus. He also had His mother and father.

Most of us experience something similar. We belong to and serve a larger community—our neighborhood, town, or city. We belong to a fellowship of believers. We have acquaintances and close friends, and then we have our intimate family or romantic relationships. And of course, our first and primary relationship is with God.

It's important for us to understand the nature of the relationships we have in our lives, because we are called to steward them well. In the next chapter, we're going to look at how we are called to love one another in our most intimate relationships.

Recommended Resources

Mims, G. *The Kingdom Focused Church.* Nashville: B&H Publishing, 2003.

Scazzerro. P. *The Emotionally Healthy Church.* Grand Rapids: Zondervan, 2010.

CHAPTER 10

MARRIAGE

But did He not make them one,
Having a remnant of the Spirit?
And why one?
He seeks godly offspring.

Malachi 2:15

One of the great themes that runs throughout the whole of the Spirit-filled life is *restoration to original design*. The Holy Spirit is committed to leading us out of a lifestyle that falls short of God's divine order, and teaching and equipping us to express His order in our thoughts, words, and actions.

The creation account in Genesis gives us a beautiful picture of God's original design for gender, sexuality, and marriage. Adam and Eve were created in God's image to share in unhindered intimacy, and in life-giving partnership. Though equals in this partnership, each brought different, complementary features to their shared assignment—to be fruitful and multiply, fill the earth, and subdue it.[75] Their relationship was to be the standard for all marriage, for all time: "Therefore a man shall leave his father and mother and be joined to his wife, and they shall become one flesh. And they were both naked, the man and his wife, and were not ashamed" (Genesis 2:24-25). Marriage is meant to be one man and one woman bonded faithfully and exclusively for life.

---

[75] Then God blessed them, and God said to them, "Be fruitful and multiply; fill the earth and subdue it; have dominion over the fish of the sea, over the birds of the air, and over every living thing that moves on the earth."– Genesis 1:28

When sin entered the picture, it had destructive effects on all aspects of this design. First, shame marred Adam and Eve's intimacy with God and with each other, causing them to hide and cover themselves. Then, their ability to be fruitful and multiply became fraught with pain and difficulty—for Adam, in his tending of the soil, and for Eve, in childbearing.[76] Their relationship with one another also shifted from a beautiful, mutual partnership to one with an imbalance of influence and power: "Your desire shall be for your husband, and he shall rule over you" (Genesis 3:16).

The narrative books of the Old Testament provide us with story after story illustrating how relations between men and women looked after the Fall. We read accounts of polygamy, sexual assault, rape, sexual slavery, harassment, adultery, divorce, and homosexuality, as well as all kinds of breakdown in the family structure in the Bible—never from a view of tolerance, but in order to show us the destructive consequences of sin, as well as God's desire to bring redemption into the midst of this broken picture.

One of the most sobering passages on marriage in the Old Testament is found in the book of Malachi. The prophet Malachi delivers a long rebuke from God to those who were breaking their marriage covenant by committing adultery:

> *You fill the place of worship with your whining and sniveling because you don't get what you want from God. Do you know why? Simple. Because God was there as a witness when you spoke your marriage vows to your young bride, and now you've broken those vows, broken the faith-bond with your vowed companion, your covenant wife. God, not you, made*

---

[76] To the woman He said: "I will greatly multiply your sorrow and your conception; in pain you shall bring forth children; your desire shall be for your husband, and he shall rule over you." Then to Adam He said, "Because you have heeded the voice of your wife, and have eaten from the tree of which I commanded you, saying, 'You shall not eat of it': Cursed is the ground for your sake; in toil you shall eat of it all the days of your life." – Genesis 3:16-17

marriage. His Spirit inhabits even the smallest details of marriage. And what does he want from marriage? Children of God, that's what. So guard the spirit of marriage within you. Don't cheat on your spouse. "I hate divorce," says the God of Israel. God-of-the-Angel-Armies says, "I hate the violent dismembering of the 'one flesh' of marriage." So watch yourselves. Don't let your guard down. Don't cheat. —Malachi 2:13-16 MSG

What this passage emphasizes is that marriage and sex are spiritual commitments—not just legal or physical. When two human beings—spirit, soul, and body—come together in a covenant and consummate that covenant through sexual union, the Holy Spirit Himself creates a new reality—a "one flesh" union, which He inhabits. This is why God considers cheating and divorce to be acts of violence against His creation. God hates divorce, and so should we.

A quick note on divorce: even though God hates it, *it happens.* I'm not saying that it *should* happen, or that God wills it to happen. However, we live in a fallen world, and Satan works overtime to poison our relationships—especially our marriages. Despite our prayers, sometimes reality doesn't line up with our expectations. Sometimes the picture-perfect marriage we imagined ends years later in tears.

So, while we should never condone divorce, we should also take it easy on condemning divorcees. The vast majority of people I know who are divorced never *wanted* a divorce. I am good friends with Christian men and women whose spouses made the decision to pursue separation because, despite best and honest efforts from both parties, the union simply didn't work. The condemnation those men and women receive from their pastors, churches, and Christian friends often adds insult to the injury those men and women have already experienced. If even Jesus did not come to condemn,[77] neither should we.

If you are divorced, know this: God still loves you more than you could ever imagine. What's more, you are *not disqualified* from ministry. The injuries you have endured will form scars that God can use to encourage others. Your testimony might be *exactly* what someone else in your church needs to hear to get through a tough time in their relationship, or their lives. None of us is perfect, but God uses us all!

Jesus' position on marriage and divorce was directly in line with Old Testament Scripture. On one memorable occasion, both the Pharisees and Jesus' disciples pushed back at Jesus' refusal to compromise on God's standard:

> *One day the Pharisees were badgering him: "Is it legal for a man to divorce his wife for any reason?"*
>
> *He answered, "Haven't you read in your Bible that the Creator originally made man and woman for each other, male and female? And because of this, a man leaves father and mother and is firmly bonded to his wife, becoming one flesh — no longer two bodies but one. Because God created this organic union of the two sexes, no one should desecrate his art by cutting them apart."*
>
> *They shot back in rebuttal, "If that's so, why did Moses give instructions for divorce papers and divorce procedures?"*
>
> *Jesus said, "Moses provided for divorce as a concession to your hard heartedness, but it is not part of God's original plan. I'm holding you to the original plan, and holding you liable for adultery if you divorce your faithful wife and then marry someone else. I make an exception in cases where the spouse has committed adultery."*
>
> *Jesus' disciples objected, "If those are the terms of marriage, we're stuck. Why get married?"*
>
> *But Jesus said, "Not everyone is mature enough to live a married life. It requires a certain aptitude and*

---

[77] For God did not send His Son into the world to condemn the world, but that the world through Him might be saved. – John 3:17

grace. Marriage isn't for everyone. Some, from birth seemingly, never give marriage a thought. Others never get asked—or accepted. And some decide not to get married for kingdom reasons. But if you're capable of growing into the largeness of marriage, do it." — *Matthew 19:3-12 MSG*

Like every other aspect of the Spirit-filled life, living out God's design for marriage requires us to become mature in Christ-likeness. The journey of "growing into the largeness of marriage" is a journey where we learn to love one particular person, day in and day out, like God loves us. As Jesus says, this journey isn't necessarily for everyone. Though we are all called to learn to love like Jesus, marriage isn't required for us to fulfill that call. However, most of us desire to be married and will marry, and so we need to know exactly what we're signing up for—God's version of marriage.

Ephesians 5: The Blueprint for Christian Marriage

If the Pharisees and disciples found God's version of marriage hard to accept, then it shouldn't be surprising that many people today struggle with accepting New Testament teaching on the subject. Much of this struggle comes from misunderstanding the language of Scripture, so it's important to push past our initial discomfort with certain terms and find out what they really mean. But even when we do understand them correctly, we are still left facing the great challenge of aligning our behavior with God's instructions. This is where we need the Holy Spirit to give us grace to trust, obey, and ultimately experience the beauty and joy of marriage as it was intended.

Let's dive right in to what may be the most beautiful yet uncomfortable passage on marriage: Ephesians 5:22-33. This is one of the most challenging texts to preach on today because it directly confronts our habit of approaching marriage with a priority on what we are getting, or going to get, out of the relationship, rather than what we are called to give. Whenever we think about marriage, we tend to think about our *rights*— What am I owed by my spouse, and how is (s)he coming up short? Instead, the apostle Paul says that we are to focus on our *responsibilities*—How can I be a better husband / wife?

Ephesians 5:22-33 covers three themes: the wife, the husband, and the union. Let's take a look at each of them.

The Wife

> *Wives, submit to your own husbands, as to the Lord. For the husband is head of the wife, as also Christ is head of the church; and He is the Savior of the body. Therefore, just as the church is subject to Christ, so let the wives be to their own husbands in everything. –*
> *Ephesians 5:22-24*

Let me state the obvious: the word "submit" makes us all extremely uncomfortable. When we think of submission, we think of inhumane treatment. We think of bending to a will that is not our own, against our wishes. I'd like to try and change the way you think about that word. The Bible is not talking about forced submission, but willing submission. The two are complete opposites.

To submit means, "to accept or yield to the will of another person." It also means "to present to a person or body for consideration." [78] When you submit, you actually position yourself to receive something favorable. In order to receive an education or be hired for a new job, you submit an application. If you want to win an award, you need to submit your name or a sample of your work to be considered. A posture of submission is necessary in almost any situation where you hope to receive something favorable, and the same is true in marriage. When a

---

[78] "submit," Google Dictionary

wife "submits," she is not bowing to the will of an abusive husband. If the husband and wife honor each other, she is actually positioning herself to receive the honor and blessing that come with a Biblical marriage.

Every wife has a very tough task in front of her, and I will be the first to acknowledge that. Submission requires complete trust. When we submit our lives to Jesus Christ, it is because we trust in Him for salvation. When wives submit their lives to husbands, they have to fully trust them.

Husbands, if you want your wife to trust you, then you need to trust her, and the Holy Spirit in her, to submit to God's design. Submission is not *your right*; it is *her responsibility*. It's not up to you to tell your wife she needs to submit to you—it's up to her to accept God's counsel and decide she needs to submit to you. All you need to worry about is becoming the best man, husband, and father you can be, and let your wife worry about following this Biblical mandate for herself. *You* need to become a God-fearing man your wife can trust with her life.

The Husband

> *Husbands, love your wives, just as Christ also loved the church and gave Himself for her, that He might sanctify and cleanse her with the washing of water by the word, that He might present her to Himself a glorious church, not having spot or wrinkle or any such thing, but that she should be holy and without blemish. So husbands ought to love their own wives as their own bodies; he who loves his wife loves himself. For no one ever hated his own flesh, but nourishes and cherishes it, just as the Lord does the church.* — *Ephesians 5:25-29*

Between the husband and wife, the former really has a tougher responsibility than the latter. Don't get me wrong—the wife has a very tough job. However, consider what God asks of husbands. God asks men to "love your wives...as Christ loved

147

the Church." What did Jesus do for His bride, the church? He *died*! He endured unending agony, suffered, and died so she could be free. Wives, your job is to submit. *Husbands, your job is to die.* I don't know about you, but submission sounds better to me!

The husband's primary responsibility is to function as the spiritual leader of his household—to model the standard of Christ's love for everyone in the family. As husbands, we need to provide an atmosphere where our wives can grow, flourish, and become whole—without spot, without wrinkle, and without blemish. We need to, "cleanse [our wives] with the washing of water by the word" (v 26). That means several things, and all of them are going to take some work: 1) the husband needs to know his Bible better than anyone else in the family, 2) he needs to be the leader when it comes to prayer (*not* just before you eat!), and 3) he needs to be the leader when it comes to displaying grace and unconditional love for everyone in his family, *especially* his wife.

Too often, the wife (mother) is the member of the household who takes spiritual responsibility for the family. Maybe dad goes out and plays golf while mom takes the kids to church. Or dad reads or watches football while mom teaches Bible stories to the kids. Whatever shape it takes, this is a trend we need to reverse.

The Promise Keepers organization published an amazing statistic:

> "When a child is the first to attend church, 3.5% of the families follow. When a wife/mom is the first to attend church, 17% of the families follow. When a dad/husband is the first to attend church, 93% of the families follow."[79]

---

[79] See PromiseKeepers.org

If we want our families to follow Biblical mandates, men (husbands and fathers) have to be the ones to commit to loving God and His Word. We have to lead by example, knowing that as we lead, our families will follow.

Jesus never forces anyone to love Him or to follow His lead. He showed His magnificent love for us in the greatest act of compassion the world has ever seen, and then allowed us to make our own decision for Him. Husbands are to treat their wives the same way. The beauty of God's design is that when both husband and wife fulfill their responsibilities, it creates a dynamic where both submitting and leading synergize and forge a deep, powerful bond in the relationship. When husbands are leading like Jesus, wives have no problem submitting; and when wives willingly show trust, husbands are inspired to lead.

The Union

Paul concludes his instructions on marriage thus:

> For we are members of His body, of His flesh and of His bones. "For this reason a man shall leave his father and mother and be joined to his wife, and the two shall become one flesh." This is a great mystery, but I speak concerning Christ and the church. Nevertheless let each one of you in particular so love his own wife as himself, and let the wife see that she respects her husband. —Ephesians 5:30-33

Paul is drawing a parallel between marriage and our relationships with Christ and the body of Christ. As we saw in the last chapter, every member of the body of Christ forms an integral part of the whole. Though each of us is unique, our uniqueness is designed to perform a critical role in the life and functioning of the body. In 1 Corinthians 12, Paul describes the attitude we should take towards ourselves and other believers due to this reality:

But now indeed there are many members, yet one body. And the eye cannot say to the hand, "I have no need of you"; nor again the head to the feet, "I have no need of you." No, much rather, those members of the body which seem to be weaker are necessary. And those members of the body which we think to be less honorable, on these we bestow greater honor; and our unpresentable parts have greater modesty, but our presentable parts have no need. But God composed the body, having given greater honor to that part which lacks it, that there should be no schism in the body, but that the members should have the same care for one another. And if one member suffers, all the members suffer with it; or if one member is honored, all the members rejoice with it. —1 Corinthians 12:20-26

Each part of the body is dependent on the healthy functioning of the other body parts. Our bodies cannot survive without the brain sending messages to every body part, to regulate functions and allocate resources and energy. We can't survive without the heart pumping blood from our core to our extremities. The same can be said for the stomach digesting food, or other internal organs processing waste.

In the same way, the marriage union requires a healthy husband and a healthy wife, working together to achieve health for the overall organism. Healthy functioning of the union is dependent on healthy functioning of both parties that contribute to the union. The husband and wife are designed as equals—but with different functions. No individual is more valuable to the union than the other, just as no body part is more valuable to the whole organism than any other. Husbands and wives each need to recognize the significance of the other and work together to achieve harmony.

Paul reminds us that we should honor members of the body of Christ who, like the hidden, weaker, or more vulnerable parts of our bodies, are the easiest to forget or ignore. The same truth is applicable to marriage. Society is set up in such a way that husbands naturally receive greater honor than wives. I'm not saying this is right; I'm just stating it's a fact, like it or not. Husbands and fathers receive accolades publicly and often; wives do not typically share that luxury.

It is important, therefore, that we honor our wives. As the head, the husband is uncovered and receives public glory. As the body, the wife is covered. As husbands, we must go out of our way to intentionally honor our wives, and make sure they receive the honor they are due. If you want your wife to invest more in your marriage, honor her more!

Finally, while husbands and wives need each other to function properly within the marriage union, they should not be ultimately dependent *on each other*. A Biblical marriage is marked by mutual dependence on Jesus Christ. A husband and wife must rely on Jesus Christ as individuals, so that when they come together in the marriage union, they will rely on Him as a couple.

The Myth of Incompatibility

As daunting, uncomfortable, and frankly unromantic (to modern sensibilities) as it seems to focus on the responsibility, submission, and leadership that marriage requires, accepting the Bible's wisdom on this point *will* pay off. God knows far better than we what will ultimately lead to our greatest health and happiness. Whenever we honor His design for our lives, we can be sure that we will benefit. Conversely, as long as we don't honor His design, we will *never* be happy.

The Bible's wisdom exposes what's broken in the way most people approach marriage in our society. All too often, both in the church community and outside it, we see people get married for the wrong reasons. The principal bad reason people get married is because they hope it will end their unhappiness. An unhappy man and an unhappy woman create an unhappy union. There is no canceling effect, as when multiplying two negatives in mathematics. Marriage is an exercise in addition. Two negatives, when added together, produce a result that is even more negative.

When you get married and expect your spouse to make you happy, you're setting both yourself *and* your future spouse up for failure. Joy and happiness are attributes only God can provide. In Psalm 16:11, David recounts to God that "…In [His] presence is fullness of joy…[and] at [His] right hand are pleasures forevermore." As finite human beings, we cannot provide for each other something that can only be provided by an infinite God. Attempting to seek happiness from our spouse is like driving a Mack truck over a bridge made out of popsicle sticks and glue. Neither the husband, nor the wife, nor the marriage union, is designed to bear that much weight. Only God can make you happy, so please don't ask your spouse to provide something he or she can never ultimately provide. It's unwise, and it's unfair.

Edwin Friedman, a family therapist and Jewish rabbi, describes something he calls the "myth of incompatibility."[80] The idea we have adopted as a society is that if marriage isn't easy, the pair involved must not be compatible. That is a good part of the reason why divorce is so prevalent. If a husband or a wife isn't happy, he or she feels the need to escape the relationship, and the court system is ready and willing to satisfy that request without batting an eye. Instead of working towards a solution, both parties hit the eject button after swallowing the lie that the marriage won't ever work between them.

Marriage is hard work. The only way it can work is if we come at it seeking sacrifice, instead of satisfaction. Jesus Christ died for the church. As husbands and wives, we must die to ourselves so we can be alive for each other. Sacrifice is the

---

[80] Friedman, E. *Generation to Generation: Family Process in Church and Synagogue.* New York: Guilford, 1985.

answer to marital bliss. Stop focusing on yourself. These questions should be banished from your thought repertoire during self-reflection: *Am I happy? Am I getting everything out of this marriage that I want to? Is my husband/wife meeting my needs?* Instead, start focusing on your spouse. What can *you* do to make your marriage better?

The Biblical model for marriage is absolutely beautiful. If you try to achieve happiness for yourself, 1) it will feel like a lot of work and 2) it will never be attainable. However, if you simply try to love and serve your spouse well, 1) it will feel effortless and 2) you will find yourself insanely happy as a by-product of your sacrifice. If a husband and a wife are constantly bending over backwards to meet each other's needs, two things will happen: they will both end up incredibly happy, and that happiness will feel absolutely effortless. Counterintuitive as this may seem, it is true. This is why Jesus said:

> *For whoever desires to save his life will lose it, but whoever loses his life for My sake will find it.* — Matthew 16:25

Jesus' message for marriage is simple: if you seek to live for yourself you will be miserable, but if you seek to live for Him you will find indescribable joy. Those are our choices in marriage as well. If you want to live to honor God, you have to start with honoring your spouse.

What If I'm Single?

As Jesus said, marriage is not for everyone. If you're reading this and you're single, please do not feel left out. God has a perfect plan for your life, and it may or may not involve a spouse. You are not *missing* anything by staying single. In fact, Paul actually told the church at Corinth, "I wish that all [were single] even as I myself" (1 Corinthians 7:7). Being single certainly has its benefits.

It also presents unique challenges. Celibacy is the most prominent challenge in single life. I fully recognize that asking young men and women to wait until marriage to have sex seems outdated, and maybe even unnatural. However, waiting until marriage is the *only* approach that honors God's design for your life and your body. God designed sex to take place inside the marriage covenant, so that husband and wife would be "naked...[but] not ashamed" (Genesis 2:25). If nakedness takes place outside of covenant, we open the door to embarrassment and shame. Just as true intimacy with God cannot take place outside of a covenant through Jesus Christ, true intimacy with a member of the opposite sex cannot take place outside of a covenant with him or her. Any attempt at intimacy without a covenant is a counterfeit.

As a single person, you will deal with temptation. I highly recommend finding a good group of Christian friends who are also single, who can encourage you and be there for you when you need it most. Ask God to give you faith that when temptation comes, God's Holy Spirit will strengthen you to endure. Most of all, know that you are *not alone*:

> No temptation has overtaken you except such as is common to man; but God is faithful, who will not allow you to be tempted beyond what you are able, but with the temptation will also make the way of escape, that you may be able to bear it. —1 Corinthians 10:13

Your "way of escape" is complete reliance on God's Holy Spirit! You cannot stay strong and resist temptation *yourself*; but God's Holy Spirit can withstand all temptation *through you*. Remembering to surround yourself with good friends, and reminding yourself that you can do "all things through Christ who strengthens [you]" (Philippians 4:13), will help you stay faithfully single.

If you do want to get married, confess your desire to God, and trust Him to lead you into marriage. Just remember that whomever you choose to marry is your choice, and that he or she is *human*. There is no such thing as a perfect spouse. Don't go chasing "the one," thinking one day a spotlight from heaven will shine down and an angel choir will start singing to announce his or her arrival. I believe God puts people of the opposite sex in your life who are marriageable candidates, and then lets you pick your spouse. That decision takes ample time in prayer, and much more input than you probably think you need from wise voices and role models in your life.

The best route to your future spouse, in my opinion, is to take steps out in the calling God has put on your life. If you're called to sing, join the worship team. If you're called to teach, join the kids ministry at your church. Do what you would normally be doing anyway; and then, once you're on your way there, look to the left, and to the right. Your future spouse might just be standing there, because (s)he has a very similar calling on his or her life.

I met my wife, Rachael, at CityLight Church. The story of how we met is really pretty, well…un-supernatural.

It started with serving. I was an usher, and she was a greeter. We both knew we were called to serve in church, and we both valued our relationship with God above everything else. We were both walking out the calling God had on our lives, with small steps of simple obedience, and gradually we started to notice each other. But nothing happened for a while. She wasn't at church to meet guys, and I wasn't there to talk to girls.

Then, one Sunday night, we had a guest minister from Australia visiting our church. After service, he asked everyone to line up for prayer. Guess whom I ended up standing next to? I turned to Rachael and dropped this super-smooth line: "Hi.

I've seen you around. Really nice to meet you." I will never forget her reply.

"I've seen you around too," she said. "You look so nice and fun!"

Sparks flew, and I proposed to her on the spot! Just kidding. In fact, I went home that night and worked up the courage to "friend" her on Facebook. But something went terribly wrong. I had set up my Facebook page in high school, and hadn't edited it since. As a bright, suburban teenager passing through his obligatory hip-hop phase, I had thought I was much cooler than I actually was. The job title on my profile read, "Ballin' full time." My employer? "Don't worry about it." (This really happened. I couldn't make this stuff up if I tried.)

Rachael accepted my "friend" request out of pity, but in the weeks following, it seemed obvious that she wanted nothing to do with me. Then one Sunday I bumped into her at church and asked how she was doing. She told me she was in the process of moving into Manhattan with her sister, Amanda, and her roommate, Stacy.

"Do you need help?" I asked.

"Sure," she said. But before she gave me more details, she offhandedly asked what I did for a living. I told her I worked on Wall Street at a major financial institution. She grinned and admitted that after seeing my Facebook profile, she had thought I was unemployed. I explained with a red face that it was a huge mistake. Eventually I asked for her number, and we picked a time to take a walk in Central Park.

I knew I would marry Rachael from that first stroll in Central Park. She is an amazing woman of God, full of joy, and indescribably beautiful. I knew she would make an incredible wife and mother, and I wanted to be the man of God in her life. She has continued to make my wildest dreams come true every day since. I am the man I am today because God sent my wife to love and support me unconditionally; and I will spend the rest of my life loving and supporting her exactly the same way.

But it all started with simple obedience: no flashing lights, and no big booming voice from heaven to guide the way. So, what is God calling you to do? Go and do it. Then, look to your left, and to your right, and say hello to the man or woman standing at your side.

Recommended Resources

Evans, J. *Marriage on the Rock.* Dallas: Marriage Today, 1994.
Keller, T. *The Meaning of Marriage.* New York: Dutton, 2011.
Köstenberger, A. *God, Marriage and Family.* Wheaton: Crossway Books, 2004.

CHAPTER 11

SERVANTS & STEWARDS

His lord said to him,
"Well done, good and faithful servant;
you were faithful over a few things,
I will make you ruler over many things.
Enter into the joy of your lord."

Matthew 25:21

"Submission" does not just belong to wives in marriage. The New Testament also instructs every believer to submit to elders and those in authority, to one another in the body of Christ, and to God. In each case, this instruction involves the same understanding—that submission is about willingly aligning ourselves with God's character and design for our lives, knowing that we are honoring Him and positioning ourselves for His favor, prosperity, blessing, and growth. Consider 1 Peter 5:5:

> *Likewise you younger people, submit yourselves to your elders. Yes, all of you be submissive to one another, and be clothed with humility, for "God resists the proud, but gives grace to the humble."*

Grace is both God's unmerited favor, and His power that enables us to live like Him. There is nothing we can do to earn His grace. All we can do is position ourselves to receive it. Ongoing grace comes into our lives as we embrace a continual posture of humility, honor, service, and generosity, just as Jesus modeled for us.

In his letter to the Philippian church, Paul gives a brilliant description of how we are to imitate the submission, humility, and willing service of Christ:

Let nothing be done through selfish ambition or conceit, but in lowliness of mind let each esteem others better than himself. Let each of you look out not only for his own interests, but also for the interests of others. Let this mind be in you which was also in Christ Jesus, who, being in the form of God, did not consider it robbery to be equal with God, but made Himself of no reputation, taking the form of a bondservant, and coming in the likeness of men. And being found in appearance as a man, He humbled Himself and became obedient to the point of death, even the death of the cross. Therefore God also has highly exalted Him and given Him the name which is above every name, that at the name of Jesus every knee should bow, of those in heaven, and of those on earth, and of those under the earth, and that every tongue should confess that Jesus Christ is Lord, to the glory of God the Father. —Philippians 2:3-11

"Humility" and "servant" are words that make us uncomfortable. We associate humility with low self-esteem, weakness, and timidity, and serving with dutiful, joyless obligation. But true humility looks like the most powerful Person in the universe boldly choosing to use His power not to serve Himself, but to save others. Jesus did not have low self-esteem. Rather, He esteemed our lives as highly as His own, and willingly sacrificed Himself on our behalf. And look where serving got Jesus—exalted to the highest place! Submission is not oppression, humility is not weakness, and serving is not joyless slavery. They are nothing less than the only path to true joy and blessing.

Becoming a Servant

In order to understand the joy of serving, we have to understand the identity, relationship, and motives of a servant.

In God's kingdom, none of His servants are slaves. They are all His sons and daughters. The chief Servant in the kingdom is the Son of God Himself. This means that the more we renew our minds in the truth of our identity in Christ and learn to think like He thinks, the more we will see serving the way He does—as the ultimate expression of greatness.

Knowing that "servant" is actually the position of greatest honor in the kingdom is a valuable test for us as we grow in maturity as sons and daughters. As we know, the Holy Spirit's assignment in our lives is to teach us to be like Jesus. He is constantly at work, convicting us of the truth that we are no longer abandoned orphans and hopeless sinners, but royal sons and daughters of the King of Kings. In everything He does, the Holy Spirit demonstrates that we are deeply loved and highly favored and esteemed by our Father, that everything He owns belongs to us, and that nothing is impossible for us in Him. Comprehending these realities is difficult enough for us, much less believing them. But when we do start to believe them, if we don't have "servant" as our goal, then it is possible for all this love, favor, and honor to go to our heads and feed an attitude of entitlement. We actually see this happen with the disciples. After hanging around and ministering with Jesus long enough, they started arguing over who was the greatest and who deserved certain honors. At this point, Jesus said, "...he who is greatest among you, let him be as the younger, and he who governs as he who serves" (Luke 22:26). Jesus didn't shut down their belief that they were great; He simply redefined what greatness looked like—serving.

The term Paul uses to describe Jesus in Philippians 2:7—"bondservant"—clues us in to the type of relationship and motives we should have as servants of God. Paul also described himself as a bondservant: "Paul, a bondservant of Jesus Christ, called to be an apostle, separated to the gospel of God..." (Romans 1:1). A bondservant was a servant who willingly elected to serve his master for his entire lifetime. According to Levitical law, the servant's choice was to be formalized through a legal procedure:

> But if the servant plainly says, "I love my master, my wife, and my children; I will not go out free," then his master shall bring him to the judges. He shall also bring him to the door, or to the doorpost, and his master shall pierce his ear with an awl; and he shall serve him forever. —Exodus 21:5-6

The bondservant relationship was a covenantal relationship based on *love*. Jesus didn't humble Himself to death because He was forced, or to earn exaltation from the Father. He did it because He loved His Father. He wanted to fulfill the Father's desire to restore His lost sons and daughters. Likewise, Paul didn't pour out his life as a missionary, enduring every form of ridicule, persecution, and physical hardship, because he was doing penance for past sins or trying to merit favor from God. He did it because He loved Jesus. Christ had won his heart and allegiance for life, and he would gladly do anything Jesus asked of him.

The life of service to which Jesus calls us can only be born out of love for God and a desire to please Him. And the only way we can love and serve God is by first receiving His love and service for us. It doesn't work any other way.

When Jesus washed His disciples' feet at the Last Supper, Peter initially refused to allow Jesus to serve him. But Jesus explained that unless Peter allowed Jesus to serve him, he couldn't be part of what Jesus was doing:

> Then He came to Simon Peter. And Peter said to Him, "Lord, are You washing my feet?"
> Jesus answered and said to him, "What I am doing you do not understand now, but you will know after this."

> *Peter said to Him, "You shall never wash my feet!"*
>
> *Jesus answered him, "If I do not wash you, you have no part with Me."*
>
> *Simon Peter said to Him, "Lord, not my feet only, but also my hands and my head!"* —John 13:6-9

The only way we can learn to be servants like Jesus is by accepting His service—by receiving His love, healing, joy, peace, instruction, provision, comfort, forgiveness, and encouragement. When we do, there is simply no way our hearts won't be captured with gratitude and passion to serve Him with all that we have and are.

Stewardship

Having the right identity, relationship, and motives are essential to fulfilling the role of a servant. Being the servant of a king is not a powerless position. In fact, it's just the opposite. Every servant of a king has a measure of access, influence, and responsibility due to his or her position. The king essentially shares his authority with his servants by trusting them to manage certain aspects of his affairs. In short, the role of every servant is stewardship. His or her job is to faithfully manage the king's resources with the king's heart, character, priorities, and principles.

As servants of our Father, we are called to steward every aspect of our lives in a way that honors and represents Him accurately. One of the first and most important areas where we must learn to be faithful is the area of money. So let's take a look at what the Bible says about financial stewardship.

Financial Submission

We don't like to talk about money in church. When it's time for the offering, some of us shift squeamishly in our seats and get uncomfortable. But did you know Jesus liked to talk about money? In fact, Jesus was so concerned with our attitude towards finances that He talked more about money than He did about heaven and hell combined. One out of every seven verses in the New Testament talks about money, and almost half of the parables Jesus told mention money! In fact, the only subject Jesus spoke about more often than money was the kingdom of God.

Jesus gave His disciples a lot to chew on in Matthew 6—the Sermon on the Mount. First, He reminded them that our priority should always be on spiritual riches, instead of physical:

> *"Do not lay up for yourselves treasures on earth, where moth and rust destroy and where thieves break in and steal; but lay up for yourselves treasures in heaven, where neither moth nor rust destroys and where thieves do not break in and steal." —Matthew 6:19-20*

Your security should never be tied to what you earn, or what you own. All your material possessions can be stolen away in an instant, and none of them will make the trip to heaven with you. So why should you spend your entire life working endlessly for something that can never truly make you secure?

Security comes from God alone. You can't buy your way into heaven with money,[81] and you can't purchase an encounter with God.[82] You could win the lottery, but still end up broke. (In fact, according to the National Endowment for Financial Education, seventy percent of lottery winners go broke within a few

---

[81] None of them can by any means redeem his brother, nor give to God a ransom for him... – Psalm 49:7

[82] And when Simon saw that through the laying on of the apostles' hands the Holy Spirit was given, he offered them money, saying, "Give me this power also, that anyone on whom I lay hands may receive the Holy Spirit." But Peter said to him, "Your money perish with you, because you thought that the gift of God could be purchased with money!" – Acts 8:18-20

years).[83] Only God can provide lasting riches. In the Psalms, David recounted, "I have been young, and now am old; yet I have not seen the righteous forsaken, nor his descendants begging bread" (Psalm 37:25). When we make a decision to serve God, He will never leave us without the resources to do His work!

Second, Jesus tells us that our spending habits reveal the orientation of our heart: "For where your treasure is, there your heart will be also" (Matthew 6:19-20). Do you want a realistic gauge of what you value most in life? Follow your money! Where do you spend the most? On what do you spend the least? If your heart is really on fire for God, it will be reflected in every aspect of your life—including how much you give towards expanding His kingdom.

Jesus warned His disciples that they would have to make a decision. Would they spend their lives working for money? Or would they spend their days working for God:

> "No one can serve two masters; for either he will hate the one and love the other, or else he will be loyal to the one and despise the other. You cannot serve God and mammon." – Matthew 6:24-25

Mammon is an Aramaic word that means wealth personified.[84] Money doesn't have to be an idol or god, but it can be—and that is when it becomes mammon. Money is not inherently bad. Scripture does not say that *money* is evil, but rather, "...the love of money is a root of all kinds of evil" (1 Timothy 6:10). When God is your master, money is just another currency God gives you to expand His kingdom—along with your words, your actions, and your prayers. But when money is your god, "all kinds of evil" come into your life. Money makes a wonderful servant, but a terrible master. So you can spend your

---

[83] http://www.nefe.org/
[84] Strong's G3126

entire life serving either God or money, but not both. You *must* make a choice. You can either serve God and take advantage of money, or serve money and allow it take advantage of you.

If you choose to serve God instead of money, He promises to *always* provide for you. Matthew 6:25-34 provides a beautiful dialogue in which Jesus reminds His disciples just how easy it is for God to provide for all of creation. God effortlessly provides for the "...birds of the air, for they neither sow nor reap nor gather into barns; yet [our] heavenly Father feeds them" (Matthew 6:26). He gracefully grows the "...lilies of the field..., [and] they neither toil nor spin" (Matthew 6:28). Are you not of more value than many birds? Are you not created to be more beautiful than a garden of flowers? You are God's most prized possession! What need do you have that He cannot meet? What request do you have that He cannot provide?

When it comes to finances, "Do not worry" is Jesus' command (Matthew 6:25, 31, 34)! We spend so much time *worrying* about God's commands to avoid sin, yet hardly any time pursuing His mandate to avoid worry! There is much work to be done for the kingdom, and worrying about finances is simply a waste of time. With Jesus as Lord of our lives, all we have to do is, "...seek first the kingdom of God and His righteousness, and all these things shall be added to [us]" (Matt 6:33)! When we seek God first, He will give us all the resources we need to fulfill the calling He has put on our lives.

At CityLight Church, we believe in Biblical prosperity. That means God will give you *more than enough*[85] to accomplish the unique calling He has put on your life. "More than enough" might have a different meaning for you than it does for your neighbor, but God is faithful to provide!

God's promise for prosperity has been warped and perverted over the years, resulting in a false line of teaching

---

[85] For more verses describing God's abundant nature, see Psalm 23:5, Matthew 17:24-27, Luke 5:6-7, and Luke 6:38.

known as the "prosperity gospel," or "name it and claim it" theology. Biblical prosperity does *not* mean you can pray for whatever you want, and God has to drop it into your lap. God is an abundantly generous Father; but He is not a genie in a bottle. Our prayers for earthly resources *must* line up with His will;[86] and when our prayers match His will, we have the petitions we have asked!

Everything we have on this earth is a gift from God. When we are faithful stewards over what He has already given us, we position ourselves to become stewards over more. How we manage our financial resources is a litmus test for how we will handle spiritual truth. It's not until we prove we can handle earthly resources that God will trust us with "true riches" (Luke 16:11).

The currency you and I work hard for every single day does us no good if our relationship with God lies in ruins. The catch is that our relationship with God cannot be fully repaired unless we give Him control over *every* area of our lives: not only *including*, but *especially* our wallets. God blessed Abraham so he could "be a blessing" to other people.[87] He will bless you for the same reason: not so you can cling to everything you receive, but so you can be a conduit to bless the people around you.

There are many biblical principles we can study to learn how to faithfully use money, but here we will focus on two: tithing and giving.

The Tithe

The term "tithe" literally means "tenth." The Bible tells us

---

[86] Now this is the confidence that we have in Him, that if we ask anything according to His will, He hears us. And if we know that He hears us, whatever we ask, we know that we have the petitions that we have asked of Him. – 1 John 5:14-15

[87] I will make you a great nation; I will bless you and make your name great; and you shall be a blessing. – Genesis 12:2

that we should give the first ten percent of our income to God.

The first instance of the tithe appears in Genesis 14. Abram rescues his nephew Lot from his captors and recovers, "...all [his] goods...as well as the women and the people" (Genesis 14:16). Immediately after the victory, Melchizedek, the king of Salem ("peace") and the "priest of God Most High" (Genesis 14:18) meets Abram at the Valley of Shaveh. He brings him bread and wine, and blesses him. In response, Abram, "...gave him a tithe of all" (Genesis 14:20). Abram knew that God had won the victory, so he honored God with a tithe (a tenth) of all the goods he had recovered, and gave that tithe to God's trusted representative.

We also see that Jacob, Abraham's grandson, adopted the tithe after God encountered him and explained that he would inherit the promises of Abraham:

> Then Jacob made a vow, saying, "If God will be with me, and keep me in this way that I am going, and give me bread to eat and clothing to put on, so that I come back to my father's house in peace, then the Lord shall be my God. And this stone which I have set as a pillar shall be God's house, and of all that You give me I will surely give a tenth to You." —Genesis 28:20-22

Hundreds of years later, the Mosaic law called for Israel to consecrate the first ten percent of all their "increase"—their agricultural produce—and give it to the temple. Israel's tithes supported the Levites, who served as the priests of the nation.

Lastly, Jesus affirmed the tithe when He criticized the Pharisees in Matthew 23:23:

> "Woe to you, scribes and Pharisees, hypocrites! For you pay tithe of mint and anise and cumin, and have neglected the weightier matters of the law: justice and mercy and faith. These you ought to have done, without leaving the others undone."

Jesus criticized the Pharisees because they tithed of their possessions, yet neglected justice and mercy. The lesson for all of us is that we should emphasize justice and mercy, without neglecting the tithe—"without leaving the others undone."

What if the Church Misuses the Funds?

When you tithe, you are physically giving to the church. Just as Abram gave his tithe to God's anointed messenger, Melchizedek, you are giving your tithes to God's anointed messengers in your local church. Spiritually, however, you are giving to God when you tithe—not man.

You might be wondering, *Doesn't that mean the tithe is just collected to support the operating budget?* Absolutely not. If God wants His house to prosper, He will make it prosper, whether you and I give towards it or not. The church is the bride of Christ—the vessel God has chosen to impact people all over the world, and the home to which all His children are called. It will continue to exist until Jesus Christ comes again, whether we invest in it or not. Any living head needs an active body to support it, and Jesus Christ certainly will not let His body wither away and die.

Your Biblical responsibility is to honor God with your tithe. When you see God face to face, that will be your end of the bargain: honoring God in response to everything He has already done to honor you. The church's responsibility is to steward those gifts wisely. Every staff member of every church who ever creates a budget or spends one single penny of church funds will be accountable for those expenses at the end of his or her life. Judgment will be more severe for those called into full-time ministry,[88] and financial responsibility should never be taken lightly. But an imperfect church, or an imperfect church budget,

---

[88] My brethren, let not many of you become teachers, knowing that we shall receive a stricter judgment. – James 3:1

does not excuse us from our individual Biblical responsibility to tithe to God.

Tithing Testimonies

The tithe exists for *your own good*. Remember, tithing conditions your heart and makes you ready to receive "true riches" (Luke 16:11). God doesn't need your money. He owns the cattle on a thousand hills;[89] in fact, He owns the hills too! He instructs us to tithe so we can learn to trust Him, and through trusting Him come to live in His blessing.

God offers His children incredible promises in the area of finances, and He actually encourages us to *test Him* in this area:

> *"Bring all the tithes into the storehouse, that there may be food in My house, and try Me now in this," says the Lord of hosts, "If I will not open for you the windows of heaven and pour out for you such blessing that there will not be room enough to receive it." —* Malachi 3:10

If you take Him at His word and start to tithe, He will change your financial picture into a reality that's better than you could have ever imagined.

John D. Rockefeller was the first billionaire in the United States. The son of an absent father and a devout Baptist mother, he rose to fame and prominence after founding the Standard Oil Company in 1870. When he died, his fortune was worth $336 billion (yes, *billion*) when adjusted for inflation. A survey by Business Insider identified him as the richest man of all time.[90] As a comparison, Bill Gates' net worth was only $136 billion in the same survey. John D. Rockefeller was a very rich man.

---

[89] For every beast of the forest is Mine, and the cattle on a thousand hills. – Psalm 50:10

[90] "The 20 Richest People Of All Time," *Business Insider*, September 2, 2010.

What does all this have to do with tithing? John D. Rockefeller wasn't just rich; the better word is *blessed*. He tithed his entire life, from his first wages to his last. Rockefeller always insisted on blessing God, and God blessed him back—immensely—as a result. John D. Rockefeller had this to say about tithing in an interview for a newspaper:

> "Yes, I tithe, and I would like to tell you how it all came about. I had to begin work as a small boy to help support my mother. My first wages amounted to $1.50 per week. The first week after I went to work, I took the $1.50 home to my mother and she held the money in her lap and explained to me that she would be happy if I would give a tenth of it to the Lord.
>
> "I did, and from that week until this day I have tithed every dollar God has entrusted to me. And I want to say, if I had not tithed the first dollar I made I would not have tithed the first million dollars I made. Tell your readers to train the children to tithe, and they will grow up to be faithful stewards of the Lord."[91]

Rockefeller used his financial blessings to bless other people. Before his death in 1937, funding from the Rockefeller Foundation led to the discovery of penicillin, along with cures for malaria, tuberculosis and diphtheria. He was blessed, and he used his God-given resources to bless others. That freedom to be blessed arose out of his decision to honor God with everything he earned.

I have seen my family's own finances completely transform as a result of tithing. I moved to New York City to start a career in finance right after graduating from college. I remember a time when I had less than $50 to my name. It was scary. My problems with money persisted until I gave that area of my life over to the Lord. God cannot bless something unless you have ceded control of it to Him.

---

[91] Tan, P. L. (1996). Encyclopedia of 7700 Illustrations: Signs of the Times. Garland, TX.

I remember hearing about the tithe at CityLight Church and thinking the idea was absolutely ludicrous. Then the church did a 30-day tithing challenge. Church leadership promised all the members that if we tithed for 30 days and didn't see our lives transformed, we could ask for all our money back. I always liked a good challenge, so I was in. And you know what? *I never asked for my money back.* In fact, not a single person at the church ever asked for his or her money back. Tithing works.

Eventually I left that career in finance to pursue full-time ministry. Believe me when I tell you that transition did *not* look good on paper. I was a Risk Arbitrage trader at a major financial institution in New York City, and I was doing well. My wife and I lived within our means, but God had stretched our means so that we weren't lacking a single thing. And then He called us to make a change.

With my wife's full support, we (because it's never about just one of you) shifted into full-time ministry. And you know what? God has provided every single step of the way. We were renting an apartment; now we own one. We had lived for years without a car because we couldn't afford it; now we drive one. We had been praying about having kids; now we have beautiful, healthy children. I had always been waiting for a calling that would satisfy me fully; now I live out that calling every single day! The decision to trust God with our finances has paid amazing dividends.

Giving: Sowing and Reaping

Paul used an agricultural metaphor to explain the reciprocal nature of generosity to the church at Corinth:

> But this I say: He who sows sparingly will also reap sparingly, and he who sows bountifully will also reap bountifully. So let each one give as he purposes in his heart, not grudgingly or of necessity; for God loves a

cheerful giver. And God is able to make all grace abound toward you, that you, always having all sufficiency in all things, may have an abundance for every good work. —2 Corinthians 9:6-8

Paul likened giving to God to sowing seed in order to illustrate several important principles: First, the quantity of seed planted determines the size of the harvest. If you need a financial breakthrough, Scripture would encourage you to plant more seed. This is counter-intuitive, because when we fall on tough times, our instincts tell us to cling to every last penny we own! But God uses the foolish things of the world to confound the wise.[92] If God knows He can get resources *through* you, He will get them *to* you. If the seed is never planted, however, the crop cannot grow. Whenever I talk with someone who is going through hard financial times, the first question I ask is, "Do you tithe?" It's amazing how many times we keep the seed in our pocket, but still expect crops to pop up out of the ground!

Second, the type of seed planted determines the type of harvest we will reap. When we give, we should expect to receive in kind. A farmer who plants corn seed in the ground is not surprised when corn stalks pop up out of the ground. However, he would never plant cucumber seeds and expect to see corn! This is why giving of your *time* isn't a substitute for your *tithe*. If you want to reap a financial harvest, you have to plant a financial seed.

Third, your motives are important. You should always, and only, be sowing to honor God. If we sow simply because we want to reap, we are giving to *ourselves* instead of to God. We must never lose sight of the ultimate purpose of our gifts: to honor God for His generosity and expand His kingdom. Charles

---

[92] But God has chosen the foolish things of the world to put to shame the wise, and God has chosen the weak things of the world to put to shame the things which are mighty... – 1 Corinthians 1:27

Spurgeon used a story of a king, a farmer, and a nobleman to illustrate this distinction (author's paraphrase):

> Once upon a time there was a king who ruled over everything in a land. One day there was a gardener who grew an enormous carrot. He took it to his king and said, "My lord, this is the greatest carrot I've ever grown or ever will grow; therefore, I want to present it to you as a token of my love and respect for you."
>
> The king was touched and discerned the man's heart, so as he turned to go, the king said, "Wait! You are clearly a good steward of the earth. I want to give a plot of land to you freely as a gift, so you can garden it all." The gardener was amazed and delighted and went home rejoicing.
>
> But there was a nobleman at the king's court who overheard all this, and he said, "My! If that is what you get for a carrot, what if you gave the king something better?" The next day the nobleman came before the king, and he was leading a handsome black stallion. He bowed low and said, "My lord, I breed horses, and this is the greatest horse I've ever bred or ever will; therefore, I want to present it to you as a token of my love and respect for you."
>
> But the king discerned his heart and said, "Thank you," and took the horse and simply dismissed him. The nobleman was perplexed, so the king said, "Let me explain. That gardener was giving me the carrot, but you were giving yourself the horse."

When we sow just for the sake of reaping, we reap nothing. But when we sow to honor the King, we will reap abundantly.

Finally, giving should be a *joyful* process. Once you know that God will meet every single one of your needs, what do you have left to worry about? If God, "…did not [even] spare His own Son, but delivered Him up for us all, how shall He not with Him also freely give us all things?" (Romans 8:32). God made provision for all your needs on the cross. We should be *cheerful* givers in response!

The blessing of the Lord makes one rich, and He adds
no sorrow with it. — *Proverbs 10:22*

I didn't fully understand the benefits of tithing until I tried it, and you might not either. But if you finally get it, give with a smile on your face and joy in your heart. The tithe, and all the blessings that come with it, are for God's people: those who choose to demonstrate their love for Him by willingly following His commandments. God is about to transform your life and bless you beyond your wildest dreams. As you demonstrate that you can be a good steward over everything God has already given into your hand, He will cause you to be steward over so much more!

Stewardship and Promotion

"Every good gift and every perfect gift is from above, and comes down from the Father of lights" (James 1:17). Since everything we have comes from God, every blessing creates a new opportunity to serve Him. If we are faithful with what God has already given us, He will give us charge over more.

Scripture notes a reward for those who use God's blessings faithfully; however, no provision is made for those who sit on their hands and let God's resources gather dust. We see this in Jesus' parable of the talents:[93]

> *"For the kingdom of heaven is like a man traveling to a*
> *far country, who called his own servants and delivered*
> *his goods to them. And to one he gave five talents, to*
> *another two, and to another one, to each according to*
> *his own ability; and immediately he went on a journey.*
> *Then he who had received the five talents went and*
> *traded with them, and made another five talents. And*
> *likewise he who had received two gained two more also.*

---

[93] A *talent* was a sum of money in first-century culture.

But he who had received one went and dug in the ground, and hid his lord's money." —Matthew 25:14-18

This passage speaks to our mandate as God's servants. Jesus has ascended to the right hand of the Father to be seated in heavenly places. After He rose from the grave, He promised to give us everything we need to continue His mission on earth. He gave us His Spirit so we could think, pray, and act like Him. He has poured out abundant material blessing on us so we can spend our energies focusing on Him. So, what are you doing with everything you've received?

It's important to note that each servant started on unequal footing. Each servant received a different amount from the beginning. Life isn't fair! Yet there was no quarreling over why one person received so much and had it made, while others received less. The mandate was simply to accept and make the most of what they had been given.

When the owner of the talents returned, he gave a reward to those who used their resources well. "Well done, good and faithful servant" (v. 21), the master said to the servant who traded his five talents to make another five. "You have been faithful over a few things, [so] I will make you ruler over many things" (v. 23), the master said to the servant who traded his two talents to make another two. But there was no reward for the servant who had hidden his talent in the ground because he was "afraid" (v. 25). The little he had was taken from him, and given to the servant with ten talents.

God has given us boldness! Why? "To grant us that we, being delivered from the hand of our enemies, might serve Him without fear" (Luke 1:74). You were not made to sit on your hands; you were made to stand on your feet, emboldened by God's promises and set free by His power. You were not given gifts from heaven to bury them in the ground, but to freely give what you have received.[94] You were made light to shine in the darkness, and the light in you cannot be hidden!

> *"Let your light so shine before men, that they may see your good works and glorify your Father in heaven."*
> *—Matthew 5:16*

Serving Others

If we are to serve God well, we must serve others. Whom do you serve in your family, or in your church? Is there someone to whom God has assigned you, to help them fulfill their calling? Choosing whom we will serve can actually be one of the most important decisions we ever make in life. Why? Because when our service is over, God actually offers us a chance to pick up that person's mantle. He offers us the chance to extend that person's calling, first through service, and then by picking up where he or she left off. It is by serving that we develop the capability to function like the people we emulate. It is through service that we become like those we serve!

We see this principle illustrated throughout Scripture. Take Moses and Joshua, for example. Moses was powerfully anointed to lead the people of Israel out of Egypt; but after Moses disobeyed one of God's commands, God told him he wouldn't be the one to lead the people into the Promised Land.[95] Some time later, God instructed Moses to train up a replacement:

> *And the Lord said to Moses: "Take Joshua the son of Nun with you, a man in whom is the Spirit, and lay your hand on him; set him before Eleazar the priest*

---

[94] Heal the sick, cleanse the lepers, raise the dead, cast out demons. Freely you have received, freely give. – Matthew 10:8

[95] Then Moses lifted his hand and struck the rock twice with his rod; and water came out abundantly, and the congregation and their animals drank. Then the Lord spoke to Moses and Aaron, "Because you did not believe Me, to hallow Me in the eyes of the children of Israel, therefore you shall not bring this assembly into the land which I have given them." – Numbers 20:11-12

and before all the congregation, and inaugurate him in their sight. And you shall give some of your authority to him, that all the congregation of the children of Israel may be obedient." — Numbers 27:18-20

One of the most critical ways in which Joshua served Moses and prepared to take the baton of leadership from him was simply spending time in God's presence. Whenever Moses met with God, Joshua was right in the room. In fact, Joshua stayed in God's presence long after Moses' time with God was over:

So the Lord spoke to Moses face to face, as a man speaks to his friend. And he would return to the camp, but his servant Joshua the son of Nun, a young man, did not depart from the tabernacle. — Exodus 33:11

When the time came for Joshua to step into a leadership role, he was prepared to communicate with God face to face, just as Moses had done. As the Book of Joshua begins, we see God speak to Joshua directly:

After the death of Moses the servant of the Lord, it came to pass that the Lord spoke to Joshua the son of Nun, Moses' assistant, saying: "Moses My servant is dead. Now therefore, arise, go over this Jordan, you and all this people, to the land which I am giving to them — the children of Israel. Every place that the sole of your foot will tread upon I have given you, as I said to Moses... as I was with Moses, so I will be with you. I will not leave you nor forsake you." — Joshua 1:1-3, 5

After many years of faithful service to Moses, Joshua inherited his mantle and access to God's presence. Because he proved he could serve faithfully and without any personal agenda, God gave Joshua the honor and responsibility of leading Israel into the Promised Land.

We see a similar progression with Elijah and Elisha. In 1 Kings 19, God told Elijah to anoint Elisha as his replacement. Years later, the time for transition arrived. Elijah was about to be pulled up into heaven, and Elisha knew it:

> *And it came to pass, when the Lord was about to take up Elijah into heaven by a whirlwind, that Elijah went with Elisha from Gilgal. Then Elijah said to Elisha, "Stay here, please, for the Lord has sent me on to Bethel." But Elisha said, "As the Lord lives, and as your soul lives, I will not leave you!" So they went down to Bethel. Now the sons of the prophets who were at Bethel came out to Elisha, and said to him, "Do you know that the Lord will take away your master from over you today?" And he said, "Yes, I know; keep silent!"* —2 Kings 2:1-3

Elisha refused to leave Elijah's side, and pledged to serve him faithfully until the very end. Finally, Elijah turned to his faithful servant and offered him whatever he would ask:

> *And so it was, when they had crossed over, that Elijah said to Elisha, "Ask! What may I do for you, before I am taken away from you?" Elisha said, "Please let a double portion of your spirit be upon me."* – 2 Kings 2:9

Elisha asked, and he received. A double portion fell upon him. He immediately picked up Elijah's mantle to perform amazing miracles. Service was Elisha's pathway to blessing.

Jesus Christ calls us into exactly the same progression. We are to read the Gospel accounts of Jesus' miracles and expect those same signs and wonders in our own lives. We are to preach the gospel, knowing that His work will follow our words. We are to pursue heaven on earth, knowing that Jesus Christ will make all the resources of heaven available to us as He sits at the right hand of the Father.

We are to serve Jesus faithfully, all of our days, until we see His Holy Spirit work *even greater* miracles through our hands:

> *"Most assuredly, I say to you, he who believes in Me, the works that I do he will do also; and greater works than these he will do, because I go to My Father. And whatever you ask in My name, that I will do, that the Father may be glorified in the Son. If you ask anything in My name, I will do it." – John 14:12-14*

God is preparing you for something greater than your wildest dreams, and more glorious than you could ever imagine. He is preparing you for transformation into the image of His Son, Jesus Christ.

Because of faithful service, Joshua walked the people of Israel into the Promised Land. He participated in the blessing originally intended for Moses, his master. Because of faithful service, Elisha received a *double portion* of the blessings Elijah experienced. And because of faithful service, we are called into greater works than even Jesus Christ was able to perform, because the same Spirit who raised Him from the dead lives in us!

Recommended Resources

White, M. *Why Should I Tithe?* New York: Intelligent Charismatic, 2015. Available at intelligentcharismatic.com / resources

CHAPTER 12

SUFFERING AND THE SPIRIT-FILLED LIFE

Therefore we do not lose heart. Even though our outward man is perishing, yet the inward man is being renewed day by day. For our light affliction, which is but for a moment, is working for us a far more exceeding and eternal weight of glory, while we do not look at the things which are seen, but at the things which are not seen. For the things which are seen are temporary, but the things which are not seen are eternal.

2 Corinthians 4:16-18

For a very long time—since sin entered the world—human beings have wrestled with the problem of suffering. Those who doubt God's existence or His goodness point to suffering in the world as proof for their position: "I can't believe a good God would allow this to happen." Meanwhile, many of those who claim to believe in God often seem to expect that serving Him should keep them from suffering—as evidenced by their disillusionment and spiritual doubt when something bad happens to them. All people—even the most mature Christians—struggle to trust God in the face of suffering.

Anything less than full trust in a good God is incompatible with the Spirit-filled life, and that must include trust in the midst of suffering. In order to build this trust, we need to embrace two mysteries: 1) that a good God has allowed suffering to enter His world and affect the people He loves, and 2) that we who have put our faith in Christ—who suffered on our behalf—still experience suffering, and God will work a specific purpose through it all.

The Origin of Suffering

Suffering was not part of God's original design when He created the earth. He never desired for sin, sickness, evil, decay, and death to infect and destroy human life. However, the freedom He gave us *did* leave open the possibility for suffering to enter His perfect world. God, who is love, made us in His image to love and be loved. Love, by definition, requires free will. And free will, by definition, means that we have another choice—the option to destroy our freedom, rather than use it as it was designed.

Tragically, that is exactly what we chose. In Genesis 1, God commissioned Adam and Eve with total freedom, power, and authority to rule the earth:

> *Then God blessed them, and God said to them, "Be fruitful and multiply; fill the earth and subdue it; have dominion over the fish of the sea, over the birds of the air, and over every living thing that moves on the earth." —Genesis 1:28*

Next, in Genesis 2, God introduced one single prohibition to their freedom, for their own protection:

> *And the LORD God commanded the man, saying, "Of every tree of the garden you may freely eat; but of the tree of the knowledge of good and evil you shall not eat, for in the day that you eat of it you shall surely die." —Genesis 2:16-17*

In Genesis 3, Satan showed up. He convinced Adam and Eve to doubt the love and goodness of God—to believe that He was lying to them and withholding good things from them. After this doubt and mistrust entered their hearts, they disobeyed the one command God had given them, and ate of the fruit from the tree of the knowledge of good and evil.

Through that one act of mistrust and disobedience, two dynamics came into play. First, the consequence God had warned them about—"you shall surely die"—entered their reality. As we saw in Chapter 1, this death was not merely physical death, but separation from the source of life Himself. Adam and Eve did not drop dead the moment they ate the fruit; rather, a curse came upon them because they had fallen out of deep communion with God. This curse brought destructive effects upon every aspect of human life, work, and relationships.

The other dynamic necessary to understand human suffering is captured in Paul's question in Romans 6:16:

> *Do you not know that to whom you present yourselves slaves to obey, you are that one's slaves whom you obey, whether of sin leading to death, or of obedience leading to righteousness?*

When Adam and Eve disobeyed God, they were actually obeying sin and sin's leader: Satan. By sinning, they broke their spiritual allegiance with God, forfeited their God-given authority over the earth to His adversary, and became that adversary's spiritual slaves. It is this enemy—"the prince of the power of the air" (Ephesians 2:2)—and his dark spiritual forces who have kept humanity in bondage to the curse of sin and death since the Fall.

Sin and spiritual bondage—these are the source of all of human suffering. This is why we live in a world where billions of people wake up every morning not knowing what they will eat, and go to sleep every night without a place to lay their heads. [96] It is why nearly 150 million people suffer from depression, nearly 1 million people commit suicide every year,

---

[96] In 2011, over one billion people—14.5 percent of the global population—were classified as "extremely poor" by the World Bank Group. "Extremely poor" is defined as making less than $1.25 per day.
http://www.worldbank.org/content/dam/Worldbank/gmr/gmr2014/GMR_2014_Full_Report.pdf. Accessed March 30, 2015.

and as many as 450 million people (over 6% of the global population) suffer from mental or behavioral disorders (this figure only accounts for those who have been properly diagnosed).[97] Sin and spiritual oppression are the source of racial strife, economic injustice, sickness, disease, war, genocide, exploitation, trafficking, crime, and every other form of social, physical, mental, emotional, and spiritual evil and suffering.

That means that we are all both victims and perpetrators of this suffering. None of us is immune to the fatal mistrust and disobedience into which Adam and Eve were tricked by Satan, or to the consequences thereof. As Paul says in Romans, "through one man sin entered the world, and death through sin, and thus death spread to all men, because all sinned" (Romans 5:12). Thus, none of us can claim to be morally superior to Adam and Eve, or to anyone else in the Bible. Adam and Eve lived in God's presence. The Israelites had a covenant with God that provided them with the best moral teaching and incredible favor and blessing. Peter and the other disciples spent three years with Jesus. Yet even with the best spiritual resources available to them, all of these people fell into deception and sinned. You and I would have done no better—perhaps even worse—in the same circumstances. The problem of sin, spiritual bondage, and suffering is a mess we got ourselves into, but cannot hope to get ourselves out of. Our only hope is a Savior.

God's Answer to Suffering

When you are confronted with the reality of human suffering, or when you are trying to bring comfort to someone who is suffering, it doesn't usually help to say, "Well, this is just another consequence of living in a fallen world!" Though this is true, it's not what really matters. What matters is God's *answer*

---

[97] www.who.int/mental_health/media/investing_mnh.pdf. Accessed 3/27/2015

to human suffering—an answer that brings unspeakable comfort, enables us to endure and overcome suffering, and helps us to understand how God's goodness and trustworthiness are revealed in our lives in the midst of suffering.

God's answer to human suffering is *Jesus*. The Father sent His Son on a mission to deal with the root cause and effects of suffering, and ultimately (in eternity) to eradicate both from the human race. This mission had two objectives: 1) to fulfill humanity's original design by living a life without sin, and 2) to bear the consequences of sin on behalf of fallen humanity. Completing these two objectives would enable God to make a great exchange—Jesus would take what we deserved so we could receive what He deserves.

Jesus' success in achieving both of these objectives is why the Bible calls Jesus Christ "the last Adam."[98] Jesus lived the sinless life Adam (and Adam's race) should have lived, and died the eternal death Adam (we) should have died. Unlike the first Adam, Jesus refused to listen to Satan's lies and demonstrated unwavering trust in and obedience to God. He then offered Himself as a perfect sacrifice to redeem us from the curse of sin and death and free us from our spiritual bondage to the devil, thus reversing both dynamics that came into play through sin and releasing a new dynamic in the earth—restoration.

Both Jesus' sinless life and perfect death required Him to suffer:

> For it was fitting for Him, for whom are all things and by whom are all things, in bringing many sons to glory, to make the captain of their salvation perfect through sufferings... —Hebrews 2:10

---

[98] And so it is written, "The first man Adam became a living being." The last Adam became a life-giving spirit. – 1 Corinthians 15:45

Though Jesus never sinned, He did suffer temptation to sin, and He suffered the consequences of *our* sin—grief, mental and emotional anguish, and physical pain and hardship:

> *Surely He has borne our griefs*
> *And carried our sorrows...*
> *He was wounded for our transgressions,*
> *He was bruised for our iniquities;*
> *The chastisement for our peace was upon Him,*
> *And by His stripes we are healed.*
> *All we like sheep have gone astray;*
> *We have turned, every one, to his own way;*
> *And the Lord has laid on Him the iniquity of us all.*
> *—Isaiah 53:4a, 5-6*

Most significantly, Jesus endured the greatest suffering that ever has been or ever will be by taking on the spiritual consequences for our sin—separation from the Father. Jesus and His Father had been together throughout eternity, their souls intertwined. As Jesus hung on the cross, that inseparable, eternal bond between Father and Son was violently ripped apart. Jesus was forsaken—cast into darkness—and suffered immeasurable pain. As the collective weight of mankind's sin fell squarely on His beaten shoulders, He bore an eternity of suffering in one infinite moment.

Hebrews says that by enduring the unimaginable horror of eternal spiritual death, Jesus took death "into himself":

> *By embracing death, taking it into himself, he destroyed the Devil's hold on death and freed all who cower through life, scared to death of death.* —
> *Hebrews 2:15 MSG*

Before the cross, human suffering was tied inextricably to the enemy's bondage, which kept us in spiritual death. On the cross, Jesus took that suffering on Himself and forever removed the enemy's right to keep us separated from the Father and under his curse. For those of us who put our faith and hope in the finished work of the cross, we can be confident that we will *never* suffer as Jesus suffered in His death. The deep pain and anguish of spiritual alienation from our Creator, and the terrifying prospect of an eternity in that state, are both forever removed from our lives.

This means that suffering before the cross and suffering after the cross look very different for believers. Yes, we do experience suffering on this side of the cross; but we no longer do so as powerless, defeated slaves who cannot hope to rise above their suffering. We do so as free sons and daughters who stand in Christ's victory over Satan—the source of all suffering; and our newfound victorious stance completely transforms how we respond to suffering and how it affects our lives. As free sons and daughters, suffering in our lives now has two basic purposes: 1) testing and proving that our faith in God is genuine, and 2) identifying us fully with Christ as we fulfill His commission to advance the gospel in the earth.

Testing of Our Faith

Hebrews 2:10 says that Jesus was made "perfect through sufferings." That word "perfect" means mature, whole, complete, and lacking nothing.[99] A few verses later, we read:

> *Therefore, in all things He had to be made like His brethren, that He might be a merciful and faithful High Priest in things pertaining to God, to make propitiation for the sins of the people. For in that He Himself has suffered, being tempted, He is able to aid those who are tempted. —Hebrews 2:17-18*

Notice that verse 18 links suffering with temptation. It also explains that Jesus took on this form of suffering for our benefit,

---

[99] Strong's G5048

so that He could aid us as we are tempted. The implication is that temptation is part of the suffering we will all experience in our lives, and that God's purpose in the midst of this suffering is to "perfect" us into mature sons and daughters, just like Jesus.

The account of Christ's temptation in the New Testament gives us valuable insight into the nature of temptation in our own lives. Let's take a look:

> *Then Jesus, being filled with the Holy Spirit, returned from the Jordan and was led by the Spirit into the wilderness, being tempted for forty days by the devil. And in those days He ate nothing, and afterward, when they had ended, He was hungry.*
>
> *And the devil said to Him, "If You are the Son of God, command this stone to become bread."*
>
> *But Jesus answered him, saying, "It is written, 'Man shall not live by bread alone, but by every word of God.'"*
>
> *Then the devil, taking Him up on a high mountain, showed Him all the kingdoms of the world in a moment of time. And the devil said to Him, "All this authority I will give You, and their glory; for this has been delivered to me, and I give it to whomever I wish. Therefore, if You will worship before me, all will be Yours."*
>
> *And Jesus answered and said to him, "Get behind Me, Satan! For it is written, 'You shall worship the Lord your God, and Him only you shall serve.'"*
>
> *Then he brought Him to Jerusalem, set Him on the pinnacle of the temple, and said to Him, "If You are the Son of God, throw Yourself down from here. For it is written:*
>
> *'He shall give His angels charge over you,*
> *To keep you,'*
> *and,*
> *'In their hands they shall bear you up,*
> *Lest you dash your foot against a stone.'"*
>
> *And Jesus answered and said to him, "It has been said, 'You shall not tempt the Lord your God.'"*
>
> *Now when the devil had ended every temptation, he departed from Him until an opportune time.*

Then Jesus returned in the power of the Spirit to Galilee, and news of Him went out through all the surrounding region. — Luke 4:1-14

When the enemy tempted Adam and Eve in the garden of Eden, he used three basic strategies. First, he tempted them to doubt the goodness of God. Second, he tempted them to doubt their identity in God. Third, he pretended to offer them what they already had as those made in God's image.[100]

We see the devil use the same strategy in the wilderness with Jesus. By inviting Jesus to force God's hand of protection, Satan tempted Him to doubt God's goodness. By demanding that Jesus prove Himself to be the Son of God, Satan tempted Him to doubt His identity. And by offering Jesus the kingdoms of the earth—which Jesus had come to reclaim on behalf of mankind as the last Adam—Satan pretended to offer Jesus the very things He was already destined to have through faithful obedience to His Father.

The enemy is cunning but unoriginal. His temptation tactics haven't changed since the Fall. As the Father's sons and daughters, we can be sure that we will be tempted in the same areas that Jesus Himself was tempted. The enemy will try to get us to doubt God's goodness, be insecure in our identity in Him, and strive to achieve for ourselves that which we can only receive from God through faith.

But there's great news for us. Jesus beat the devil, and He is fully committed to helping us beat him too. The temptation account shows us two of Jesus' best strategies for resisting temptation. First, Jesus fasted and prayed. He completely emptied Himself of physical strength and immersed Himself in

---

[100] Now the serpent was more cunning than any beast of the field which the Lord God had made. And he said to the woman, "Has God indeed said, 'You shall not eat of every tree of the garden'?"...Then the serpent said to the woman, "You will not surely die. For God knows that in the day you eat of it your eyes will be opened, and you will be like God, knowing good and evil." – Genesis 3:1, 4-5

the presence of God so He would be positioned to depend fully upon God for victory. Second, Jesus did not attempt to reason or argue with the devil on His own. He stood firmly and solely on the word of God.

A lifestyle of prayer, fasting, and study and meditation in the Scriptures is not just something every Spirit-filled believer should pursue because it's a good idea; it is life-and-death training and preparation to face temptation like Jesus and with Jesus. Notice that the devil can also quote Scripture. Jesus knew the Bible better than the devil, and so must we.

Also, notice that Jesus' entire temptation experience began and ended with the Holy Spirit's guidance. Jesus was filled with the Spirit, led by the Spirit, and came out of the wilderness in the power of the Spirit. The same is to be true for us. Does that mean the Holy Spirit leads us into temptation? No—Jesus taught us to pray just the opposite.[101] James also gave a clear instruction on this point: "Let no one say when he is tempted, 'I am tempted by God'; for God cannot be tempted by evil, nor does He Himself tempt anyone" (James 1:13). God is not the author of temptation, just as He is not the author of sin or suffering; but He works in the midst of those things to bring about His ultimate plan for us. Specifically, He limits the intensity of temptation, and provides an escape route through it:

> No temptation has overtaken you except such as is common to man; but God is faithful, who will not allow you to be tempted beyond what you are able, but with the temptation will also make the way of escape, that you may be able to bear it. —1 Corinthians 10:13

The writers of the New Testament clearly understood the endgame God had in mind for His sons and daughters as they suffered temptation, testing, and trials. The prize at stake in

---

[101] And do not lead us into temptation, but deliver us from the evil one. – Matthew 6:13a

every test is our faith—our allegiance to and relationship with God. When the enemy tempts us to lie, lust, hold a grudge, feed jealousy, entertain hopelessness, care more about people's opinions than God's, or indulge in any other type of sin, the question we are really being asked is: "Do you really trust God? Do you trust His Word? Do you believe He is who He says He is? Do you believe you are who He says you are?" When we give in to temptation, we are saying, "God, I don't trust You." But when we choose to stand firm in faith, unwavering in our allegiance to God, we don't just barely make it out alive on the other side of the temptation. Our identity in God and our intimacy with Him grow deeper and stronger. We become more "perfect"—we have more of Him, and are more of ourselves in Him.

With our faith at stake, the New Testament writers urge us to have two specific attitudes toward temptation. First, we are to remain sober-minded and watchful, guarding against distractions or spiritual dullness:

> Be sober, be vigilant; because your adversary the devil walks about like a roaring lion, seeking whom he may devour. Resist him, steadfast in the faith, knowing that the same sufferings are experienced by your brotherhood in the world. But may the God of all grace, who called us to His eternal glory by Christ Jesus, after you have suffered a while, perfect, establish, strengthen, and settle you. —2 Peter 5:8-10

Paul underscores this point by reminding us that Satan does not wage his war against us on the physical plane, but on the battlefield of our minds:

> For though we walk in the flesh, we do not war according to the flesh. For the weapons of our warfare are not carnal but mighty in God for pulling down strongholds, casting down arguments and every high thing that exalts itself against the knowledge of God,

> *bringing every thought into captivity to the obedience
> of Christ... —2 Corinthians 10:3-5*

Being sober and vigilant means taking *every thought* captive. Think about how many thoughts you think in a day. The journey to becoming mature sons and daughters requires us to develop a heightened awareness of what is going on in our minds at all times. This does not mean we are to be fearful or hyper-vigilant. Fear empowers the enemy. We must never forget that we are seated in heavenly places in Christ and have full authority over the enemy. [102, 103] In Christ, we have nothing to fear.

Second, we are to *rejoice* in the face of trials and temptation— not because of the trials, but because of the result God will bring as we persevere through them:

> *My brethren, count it all joy when you fall into
> various trials, knowing that the testing of your faith
> produces patience. But let patience have its perfect
> work, that you may be perfect and complete, lacking
> nothing. —James 1:2-4*

> *In this you greatly rejoice, though now for a little
> while, if need be, you have been grieved by various
> trials, that the genuineness of your faith, being much
> more precious than gold that perishes, though it is
> tested by fire, may be found to praise, honor, and glory
> at the revelation of Jesus Christ... —1 Peter 6-7*

Rejoicing when you are "grieved by various trials" seems counterintuitive. But God is not telling us to pretend we're happy when we're not. He is giving us an invaluable key to

---

[102] ...even when we were dead in trespasses, [God] made us alive together with Christ (by grace you have been saved), and raised us up together, and made us sit together in the heavenly places in Christ Jesus... – Ephesians 2:5-6

[103] Behold, I give you the authority to trample on serpents and scorpions, and over all the power of the enemy, and nothing shall by any means hurt you. – Luke 10:19

enduring and overcoming suffering. In order to rejoice in God in the midst of suffering, we have to focus on Him. We have to turn our eyes away from the pain and the problem and let Him fill our field of vision. As we remember who He is and all He's done for us, our pain is relieved by His comforting, reassuring presence, and our problem becomes dwarfed by the size of our Solution. We gain fresh perspective and fresh strength for the fight, for "the joy of the Lord is [our] strength" (Nehemiah 8:10).

Advancing the Gospel

Joyfully enduring testing and temptation refines and matures us as sons and daughters of God. Maintaining joy through suffering not only inspires internal spiritual formation; it also forces external change that conditions us to more effectively advance the gospel with our words and actions.

Paul described the reality of the gospel in our lives as a fragrance we give off wherever we go:

> *Now thanks be to God who always leads us in triumph in Christ, and through us diffuses the fragrance of His knowledge in every place. For we are to God the fragrance of Christ among those who are being saved and among those who are perishing. To the one we are the aroma of death leading to death, and to the other the aroma of life leading to life.* —*2 Corinthians 2:14-16*

The image is clear—the gospel attracts those who are being drawn to Christ by the Spirit, and repels those who are locked in spiritual bondage. This is why we face persecution for the gospel in the world.

Jesus actually guaranteed persecution would come to His disciples: "Remember the word that I said to you, 'A servant is not greater than his master.' If they persecuted Me, they will also persecute you. If they kept My word, they will keep yours also" (John 15:20). We are called to endure persecution for the sake of the gospel.[104]

Throughout the New Testament, we find that the early church actually viewed persecution as a positive sign that they were fully identifying with Jesus and obeying His commission to preach the gospel:

> ...when [the Jewish religious council] had called for the apostles and beaten them, they commanded that they should not speak in the name of Jesus, and let them go. So they departed from the presence of the council, rejoicing that they were counted worthy to suffer shame for His name. —Acts 4:40-41

Likewise, Paul called it a pleasure to suffer for Christ's sake:

> Therefore I take pleasure in infirmities, in reproaches, in needs, in persecutions, in distresses, for Christ's sake. For when I am weak, then I am strong. —2 Corinthians 12:10

Does that make Paul a masochist? I think not. He simply understood that enduring these things "for Christ's sake" made room for the power of the gospel to be demonstrated and seen through his life.

We are all called to give our lives for the gospel. For some Christians around the world, this may mean actual martyrdom, just as it did for the all but one of Jesus' disciples (John) and many other saints in the early church. In more tolerant places of the world, like the United States, your chances of being martyred are much lower. However, it's not hard to identify persecution in Western Culture—places where the gospel and those who believe in it are mocked, derided, written off, or even angrily opposed. This is where we need to pay attention to

---

[104] But *only* for the sake of the gospel (Mark 10:29)! We are not called to endure suffering for the sake of pious outward appearance. To understand the difference, please see the next section titled, "Ungodly Suffering."

everything Jesus taught and the disciples modeled about how to respond to persecution. We 1) shouldn't be surprised, 2) should rejoice and be encouraged, and 3) should continue preaching and living the gospel with even more passion and boldness.[105]

Ungodly Suffering

It is possible and even common for Christians to suffer in ways that don't align with God's purpose or will for suffering in our lives. It's important for us to understand what these are so we can recognize and avoid them.

First, some Christians look at any bad thing happening in their lives and call it suffering for Christ, even when it's not strengthening their faith or advancing the gospel. Paul took "pleasure" in suffering "for Christ's sake" (2 Corinthians 12:10). Peter said he was "blessed" to suffer "for righteousness' sake" (1 Peter 3:14). Jesus said there is a reward for all those who endure suffering, "...for [His] sake and the gospel's" (Mark 10:29). But when we endure unnecessary suffering without actually advancing the gospel—even if it makes us look "holy" or "pious" to our neighbors—we fall into error.

If your suffering does not further your intimacy with God or the gospel message in any way, shape, or form, it is not something you are called to bear. And if you're bragging about how much you're sacrificing for Jesus, then you simply don't have a handle on what He sacrificed for you, nor do you recognize that any sacrifice for Him is worth nothing in comparison to everything He has done for you:

> So Jesus answered and said, "Assuredly, I say to you, there is no one who has left house or brothers or sisters or father or mother or wife or children or lands, for My

---

[105] And when they had prayed, the place where they were assembled together was shaken; and they were all filled with the Holy Spirit, and they spoke the word of God with boldness. – Acts 4:31

sake and the gospel's, who shall not receive a hundredfold now in this time—houses and brothers and sisters and mothers and children and lands, with persecutions—and in the age to come, eternal life." —
Mark 10:29-30

Second, Christians often place too much of a priority on suffering and expect it to be the normal state of their lives—as though suffering in itself is somehow holy. *Suffering* is not holy; but God will make *us* holy through suffering. He will also make us holy through His kindness, goodness, and joy. Like any good father, our Heavenly Father does not take pleasure in seeing His sons and daughters suffer. He wants to relieve suffering, grow us through suffering, and ultimately lead us out of suffering and into joy.

One of the biggest problems with this second erroneous view of suffering is that it goes so far as to make God the author of suffering in our lives. Satan—not God—is the author of suffering. The church is plagued with the notion that God Himself brings hardship, sickness, and disease on His people to teach us a lesson. But Jesus directly refuted that notion:

"Every kingdom divided against itself is brought to desolation, and every city or house divided against itself will not stand." —Matthew 12:25

Why would Jesus spend His entire earthly ministry eradicating sickness and disease, and defeating Satan, only to have God give us over to the devil and his devices in the end? He would not. He *could* not.

Many people use the Book of Job as Biblical proof that God authorizes suffering in the lives of believers. But what we actually read in Job 1 is that Satan is the author of Job's suffering, not God:

Now there was a day when the sons of God came to present themselves before the Lord, and Satan also came among them. And the Lord said to Satan, "From where do you come?" So Satan answered the Lord and said, "From going to and fro on the earth, and from walking back and forth on it." Then the Lord said to Satan, "Have you considered My servant Job, that there is none like him on the earth, a blameless and upright man, one who fears God and shuns evil?" So Satan answered the Lord and said, "Does Job fear God for nothing? Have You not made a hedge around him, around his household, and around all that he has on every side? You have blessed the work of his hands, and his possessions have increased in the land. But now, stretch out Your hand and touch all that he has, and he will surely curse You to Your face!" And the Lord said to Satan, "Behold, all that he has is in your power; only do not lay a hand on his person." So Satan went out from the presence of the Lord. —Job 1:6-12

God gave Job into Satan's hand because there was no mediator to shut down the transfer process. Job was living under the Old Covenant. However, as part of our New Covenant with God, Jesus now serves as our Mediator:

For there is one God and one Mediator between God and men, the Man Jesus Christ... —1 Timothy 2:5

Jesus is now seated next to God, advocating for us to the Father. If Satan ever asks for us the way he asked for Job, *God will no longer say yes.* Satan can ask for us as much as he wants; but under the New Covenant, Jesus stands between Satan and God to put up His hand and say, "I don't think so! Not on my watch."

We see this principle play out with Peter in Luke's Gospel account:

And the Lord said, "Simon, Simon! Indeed, Satan has asked for you, that he may sift you as wheat. But I have prayed for you, that your faith should not fail;

and when you have returned to Me, strengthen your
brethren." —Luke 22:31-32

Satan asked for Peter, just as he asked for Job. But whereas Job was left defenseless, Peter had a Mediator to step in and *pray for him.* Jesus' response will be the same for every single one of us when we call on His name!

Though Job remained faithful to God through his suffering, he wasn't equipped to endure suffering as we can. Job never identified Satan as his adversary. He spent *forty-two chapters* crying out to God and wondering why his life had fallen apart. But we can and should know our enemy, as well as how to defeat him. Jesus has given us, "...authority to trample on serpents and scorpions, and over all the power of the enemy..." (Luke 10:19). We can rebuke Satan in the name of Jesus. Because of the power in His name, we have the means to overcome all the suffering the enemy wants to put us through!

Most significantly, Job did not remain in suffering! At the end of the Book of Job, God restored everything to Job:

> *And the Lord restored Job's losses when he prayed for*
> *his friends. Indeed the Lord gave Job twice as much as*
> *he had before. —Job 42:10*

All of Job's friends thought Job's suffering was from God. They erroneously adopted retribution theology: the idea that if you're experiencing something bad in your life, it's because you did something wrong. Job's friends completely missed the point: Satan caused the whole disaster in the first place! Job had to pray for his friends, and correct their theology of suffering, before God could restore everything to him. When we meet Christians who fail to understand that suffering is not from God, it is our responsibility to do the same! Job poses the question of why suffering exists, but Jesus is the answer of what to do about it.

The Joy

One of the quickest ways to make sure your perspective on suffering is aligned with God's is to do a "joy check." Hebrews tells us:

> Therefore we also, since we are surrounded by so great a cloud of witnesses, let us lay aside every weight, and the sin which so easily ensnares us, and let us run with endurance the race that is set before us, looking unto Jesus, the author and finisher of our faith, who for the joy that was set before Him endured the cross, despising the shame, and has sat down at the right hand of the throne of God. —Hebrews 12:1-2

The same joy that was set before Jesus is set before you. It is the joy of being fully reconciled and united with a loving Father and partnering with Him to reconcile more beloved sons and daughters to Him. If you are not experiencing this joy and feeling compelled, as Jesus was, to run after it, no matter what suffering or sacrifice it requires, then it's time to press in and ask the Holy Spirit to give you His joy! This is the joy of the Spirit-filled life. This joy, not suffering, is to be your new normal.

Recommended Resources

Keller, T. *Walking with God through Pain and Suffering.* New York: Penguin, 2015.

CONCLUSION

When I was ten years old, my family spent a week's vacation at a camp in Upstate New York. A day or two into the vacation, someone at the camp encouraged us to go on a rafting trip on the Hudson River. I was right at the minimum age to go, which made my parents (and me!) a little nervous. We had heard horror stories about kids being thrown from the boat into the churning rapids; in fact, someone had drowned only two months before. But the owner of the camp assured us I would be fine, so we accepted the risk and said yes to the adventure.

As we arrived at the river, I could feel my heart beating fast with a mix of fear and anticipation. We met the guide who would be taking us down the rapids, and he assured us he knew what he was doing. Yes, the rapids were extreme (Class IV!), but he had been down this section of the river hundreds of times before, and knew it like the back of his hand. If we listened to his instructions, he assured us, we would have the time of our lives. We strapped on helmets and life vests, chose paddles, climbed into the raft, and pushed out into the river.

"Left!" the tour guide yelled. Obediently, we all dug our paddles into the water on the left side of the raft.

"Hard right!" he called next. We all switched our stances and dug in our paddles on the right side of the boat.

We passed successfully through several small sets of rapids, working as a team to steer the boat around large rocks jutting out of the water, all the while getting acclimated to the fast current. We were getting the hang of it. My brother and I looked at our parents. We were all grinning ear-to-ear. "This is awesome!" I yelled, the sound of my voice echoing off the majestic 500-foot granite cliffs that flanked the Hudson River on both sides.

As we looked up to admire our surroundings, we saw God's creation on full display. Crystal-clear water ran swiftly all around us as we rushed past large cedar trees and exposed rock faces. An occasional hawk circled overhead, soaring effortlessly in the cool blue sky. Soft, white clouds danced above us, and the warm sun softly baked our skin.

After almost an hour on the river, we heard the sound of fierce rushing water ahead.

"This is the big one!" the tour guide shouted.

We were approaching the largest set of rapids on this trip, and one of the most tumultuous on the Hudson River. This was the adventure we were looking for!

As we came around the next bend of the river, the roaring rapids came into full view. Our jaws dropped. The water ahead of us was white with foam as it churned in and out of ravines, over visible rock outcroppings and even fallen trees. It was hauntingly beautiful—like nothing I had ever seen before.

We caught sight of several rafts ahead of us struggling to make it through the rapids. We watched as one of them rammed hard into a rock. All the passengers lurched forward, looking like they had the wind knocked out of them. They slid slowly off the slimy rock and continued down the rapids backwards, with everyone on board visibly shaken.

Our guide reassured us we would be fine. He drew the ideal route for us in the air with his finger, then let out an excited yell as we started down the rapids. We lurched over a big wave, crashed down over what felt like a small waterfall, and careened into the same boulder the boat ahead of us had hit. THUD! I closed my eyes and braced for impact. But the impact never came.

When I opened my eyes, I was flying through the air, my ten-year-old arms flailing and grasping to grab hold of anything within reach. Then I splashed into the cold, wild water.

"Mom! Dad! Chris!" I cried out, gasping and spluttering. Panic swept through me as I saw the raft moving away from me at breakneck speed down the rapids. My parents were looking back at me in horror, their eyes wide with fear.

"Michael!" my mom screamed, trying to stand up and reach for me. She almost lost her balance and fell into the waves before my dad could grab her and pull her back into the boat. I could see tears in her eyes and feel them welling up in my own. I was alone, and I was afraid.

But our guide had told us what to do if we fell in the water. "Remember what he said," I told myself. I crossed my arms over my chest and put my feet in front of me, struggling to keep my legs pointed downstream to block my body from anything I might run into. The water carried me swiftly forward through the next set of rapids. I tried to keep my eyes open, but wave after wave of river water washed over my face. Then, my body thudded into something hard. SMACK! The rapids had carried me right into another giant boulder. Pain shot up my left arm, but I somehow found a hand-hold on the rock, and scrambled up onto it.

I stood up on the rock and examined my body. Nothing looked broken. Blood was pouring down my left hand, and I saw a chunk of skin was missing from one of my knuckles. But the blood was quickly washed away by the river water dripping off my arm. I could feel adrenaline coursing through my veins. I was safe. I was alive!

After standing on the rock for several minutes, I saw another raft coming down the rapids. I waved my hands and their guide stood and waved back. "Stay there!" he yelled to me, and then screamed "PUSH!" at everyone in his boat. Their raft made its way towards me, and soon scraped up onto the boulder where I was standing. I hopped in the boat, right into the arms of the guide. "We'll get you back to your boat," he assured me.

A few minutes later, we spotted my family waiting for us downstream. I waved as we approached, assuring them I was okay. When I finally got to my parents, I jumped into their arms. Then I thanked the guide for carrying me safely through. I was shaken up, but I was safe. Everything was going to be just fine.

Perfect Peace

God's Holy Spirit is often described as a river in Scripture:

> *On the last day, that great day of the feast, Jesus stood and cried out, saying, "If anyone thirsts, let him come to Me and drink. He who believes in Me, as the Scripture has said, out of his heart will flow rivers of living water." —John 7:37-38*

Living "in the river" entails constant motion and forward progress. No longer will you be required to push forward and fight stagnancy on your own. Instead, God will lift you up and carry you forward in the current of His Word. Life with Jesus as your Guide should be incredibly refreshing, as the Word of God "washes over you" (Ephesians 5:26).

But life in the Spirit can also be bumpy and unpredictable. You are pushing off into new waters that are fresh and living, but often tumultuous. You're stepping off the shores of safe, religious interaction with God, and braving the rapids. Once you're in the boat, life will take unexpected turns. You may be led down steep ravines and uneven terrain. You may even be thrown out of the boat! But with great risk comes great reward.

You will hear stories of people who have been tossed from the boat, but don't let them scare you. Those who have never been down the river will try and entice you to stay on shore with them, watching as life rushes by. But you must press forward.

The Spirit-filled life will take you places you don't expect, and present you with obstacles you cannot possibly predict. But God will equip you to weather every storm. You are armed with the helmet of salvation, and buoyed by His breastplate of righteousness.[106] God's express purpose is to keep you protected as you pass through life's unexpected moments, and to work "all things" together for your good (Romans 8:28).

Jesus is a good Guide. God has done this many times before. He will get you through the scariest sets of raging rapids in one piece. As the Holy Spirit carries you downstream, He will "guide you into all truth" (John 16:13). And at the end of the day, you will be better for it—stronger, more courageous, and more fearless than ever before. You will be perfected, and ready to be delivered into the arms of your loving Father.

---

[106] "Stand therefore, having girded your waist with truth, having put on the breastplate of righteousness... And take the helmet of salvation..." — Ephesians 6:14, 17a

SCIENCE & FAITH

Science has brought overwhelming benefits to society and humanity. Doctors and researchers have made amazing discoveries that have led to the complete eradication of countless once-deadly diseases. Because physicians have studied nutrition, whole countries have escaped from hunger.

Unfortunately, the popular notion today is that science and religion are at odds. I completely disagree.[107] Doctors can reveal the wonder of God's creation just as easily as pastors and teachers. God can work miracles through the hands of physicians just as easily as apostles. However, we must always recognize that God is the Divine Physician. Scientists and researchers never *invent* anything; they simply *discover* what God has already invented. Everything that exists has been put here by God. Just because we discover something that was previously not understood does not mean that we created it.

Scientific discovery has become synonymous with "fact." In light of this, we must be particularly careful to examine information before we accept it as true. Unfortunately, over the years we have developed the tendency to hear some new "scientific proof" in conversation, which we then immediately take as "fact." We don't examine the evidence at all, and what was just simple rhetoric over a cup of coffee or overheard somewhere suddenly becomes a firmly-held belief.

The legal process is very different from the scientific process. In the legal system, there is a concept called the burden of proof. When someone is accused of a crime, the burden of proof falls

---

[107] Many prominent theologians and scientists also share my view that science and religion are compatible. Please see the recommended resources at the end of this chapter for more.

on the prosecution. The accused is innocent until proven guilty, and in order for guilt to be established, the prosecution (i.e. the accuser) must prove that (s)he has credible evidence that the accused is guilty. There are various standards of proof required depending on the case: sometimes proof must be established beyond a reasonable doubt, but other times less conclusive evidence will stand. The accusation cannot be established as fact until there is conclusive evidence in support of it.

Science works much the opposite way. There is no standard equivalent to the legal concept of, "innocent until proven guilty." In science, a theory must not be *proved* to be taken as fact. Instead, any theory can be proposed, and will stand as "fact" unless it can be *disproved*. Instead of starting at ground level and establishing relevant facts to reach a conclusion based on the information at hand, science starts at a theory (i.e. a potential conclusion) and waits for a team of researchers to shoot the theory down. Until and unless it is disproved, the theory is taken as fact.

This is why it is impossible to disprove so many scientific theories about our nature as human beings, as well as the history of the earth. Darwin's theory of evolution will probably never be disproved, because there is no conclusive evidence that can ever disprove it. It is a theory, an idea. But there will also never be any evidence that will conclusively *prove* it, either. This is the difference between the legal system and the scientific community. Whereas lack of *proof* in the court system would mean a claim cannot be established, lack of *disproof* in the scientific community means a theory is free to stand as fact. This holds not only for evolution, but also for questions that have confounded Christians for generations, such as "How old is the earth?" and "What about the dinosaurs?"

My dad taught me a very important lesson when I was little. Whenever I would make a statement I understood to be "fact," he would ask me what evidence I had to support my conclusion.

Sometimes I got a little annoyed. Did he expect me to research every single statement I ever made? But he had a valid point. So often, we start sentences with statements such as, "Science has proven...," or "Everybody is saying...," without really determining if we have factual basis to make that statement in the first place! Making unsubstantiated assumptions and statements can be harmful—not only to us, but also to the people around us.

Again, I am not discounting science at all. I love science. It is a gift God has given to man for our own benefit. There are many scientific theories that have been tried and tested, and have stood because overwhelming evidence supports a hypothesis. But there are many more that lack that level of evidence, and don't deserve to be treated with the same level of trustworthiness.

We must carefully examine the information at hand before we take it as "fact." This is particularly relevant in an age where scientists are making efforts to "prove" that unnatural characteristics like homosexuality can be inherited. There is no conclusive evidence that proves that theory; in fact, much of the evidence established and published has since been discredited.[108] Use your head to protect your heart, and think things through before you establish some vague notion as "scientific fact."

Questions Science Can't Answer

There are certain questions in life that cannot be answered

---

[108] There is no "gay gene." Even the American Psychological Association (APA), which has a history of being a liberal scientific community, states: "There is no consensus among scientists about the exact reasons that an individual develops a heterosexual, bisexual, gay or lesbian orientation. Although much research has examined the possible genetic, hormonal, developmental, social and cultural influences on sexual orientation, no findings have emerged that permit scientists to conclude that sexual orientation is determined by any particular factor or factors."
From http://www.apa.org/topics/lgbt/orientation.aspx

with scientific evidence. Examples include:

- What is the meaning of life?
- Does God exist?
- What happens to me when I die?

It is for this reason that we must be very honest about exactly what type of question we are asking. When it comes to an issue like homosexuality, for example, science certainly may be able to prove that a certain gene (or many genes) are *correlated* with homosexual tendencies. However, correlation does not prove causation.

The question, "Is someone born a homosexual?" can never be answered by science. This is no longer a question of evidence; it is a question of *design*. And in order to answer that question, scientists must presume they have a vantage point that allows them to determine what mankind was designed to do. In other words, any scientist answering such a question is attempting to answer a theological question with scientific information. Such an answer can never satisfy such a question.

This is where faith comes in. The following verse is foundational to our understanding of what exactly constitutes "evidence" when it comes to theological questions and answers:

> *Now faith is the substance of things hoped for, the evidence of things not seen. —Hebrews 11:1*

Faith is the evidence of things we can't yet see, and the substance (tangible proof) of things for which we are hoping. When I make a statement such as "God exists," it can never be based on scientific fact. It must be based on faith. I know there is a God because of experience; not because of scientific proof. God has made Himself real to me on many occasions, and His gospel message has transformed my life in ways too numerous to count.

I have seen people miraculously healed of terminal diseases as a result of prayers of faith. Many of these people have had their healing confirmed by physicians. But the existence of God can never be proved beyond the shadow of a doubt according to what science deems to be "fact."

That being said, we should *always* examine the evidence of any supernatural claim. If someone claims to be healed, I want to see proof. The Bible encourages this search for evidence. When Mary and the other women at the tomb told Peter and John about the Resurrection, they dropped everything and ran to examine the evidence:

> *Then the other disciple, who came to the tomb first, went in also; and he saw and believed.* —John 20:8

This verse tells us that he (1) saw the evidence, and (2) immediately believed. John had yet to see the risen Christ for himself; yet he was able to examine the evidence he already had and make a faith decision at that moment.

Each and every single one of us is in a similar situation. Unless you have been blessed with some miraculous encounter in which Jesus Christ Himself appeared to you in a vision or a dream, you have probably not seen Him face to face. Yet we are still required to make a decision as to what exactly we believe, based on the evidence we already have in front of us. This is not unfair; it is actually exactly what God requires.

We see this in the account of "doubting" Thomas. When the disciple Thomas heard the testimony of Christ's resurrection, he said, "Unless I see in His hands the print of the nails, and put my finger into the print of the nails, and put my hand into His side, I will not believe" (John 20:25). When Jesus appeared to the disciples a week later, He offered Thomas the evidence he had demanded: "Reach your finger here, and look at My hands; and reach your hand here, and put it into My side. Do not be unbelieving, but believing" (John 20:27). Unsurprisingly, Thomas responded to Jesus in that moment with faith. Then Jesus made this statement: ""Thomas, because you have seen Me, you have believed. Blessed are those who have not seen and yet have believed" (John 20:29). Jesus was not saying that we cannot encounter Him for ourselves, or that living without encounters is somehow more spiritual. He was saying that we are blessed when we can believe in Him through the testimony of other people's encounters.

We have a complete account of the life of Jesus Christ from four different Spirit-filled authors. On top of that, millions of believers have left accounts of all the awe-inspiring things Jesus has done in their own lives. God does not leave open to us the option of waiting until we see Him face to face to make a decision as to whether or not we believe in Him; He asks us to use the evidence we already have in front of us and decide, here and now, to believe in His Son Jesus Christ.

There is no reward for waiting to believe in Christ until we see Him, whether after we die or at His second coming. By then it will be too late. Infinite reward is reserved for those who make the choice to believe in Jesus while we are still alive.

Jesus Knows

In Luke 8, a religious ruler named Jairus begs for Jesus to heal his daughter. Jesus encouraged him to have faith, and agreed to come see her. As Jesus traveled, however, the man's daughter died. Still, Jesus continued on the way to his home.

When Jesus arrived at Jairus' house to raise his daughter from the dead, everyone ridiculed Him. They "knew" she was dead. Her death had become a scientific fact. But Jesus knew otherwise.

What have you accepted as fact? Do you believe your doctors, or do you know God heals?[109] Do you believe your bank account statement, or do you know God will open up the windows of heaven and pour out on you such blessing that there will not be room enough to contain it?[110]

To "know" can have two meanings. First, we can *know* something through observation: according to all the onlookers, Jairus' daughter was dead. Or, we can *know someone* through relationship. As we learn to trust in Jesus, He will prove He is capable of everything God's word says He is.

God is not mocked.[111] He is willing to upend everything you think you *know* just to prove that He knows best. He will force you to abandon everything you have digested as fact, in favor of feasting on His Word.

Nothing is impossible with God. Will you let Him prove it to you?

Recommended Resources

Lewis, C. *Miracles.* New York: Harper Collins, 1996.

Metaxas, E. *Miracles: What They Are, Why They Happen, and How They Can Change Your Life.* New York: Plume, 2015.

Polkinghorne, J. *Science and Religion in Quest for Truth.* New Haven: Yale University Press, 2012.

Ross, H. *More Than a Theory: Revealing a Testable Model for Creation.* Grand Rapids: Baker, 2012.

---

[109] But He was wounded for our transgressions, He was bruised for our iniquities; the chastisement for our peace was upon Him, and by His stripes we are healed. – Isaiah 53:5

[110] "Bring all the tithes into the storehouse, that there may be food in My house, and try Me now in this," says the Lord of hosts, "If I will not open for you the windows of heaven and pour out for you such blessing that there will not be room enough to receive it." – Malachi 3:10

[111] Do not be deceived, God is not mocked; for whatever a man sows, that he will also reap. – Galatians 6:7

Changing the way you think about your faith.

For more resources, please visit
intelligentcharismatic.com.

Made in the USA
Middletown, DE
09 August 2017